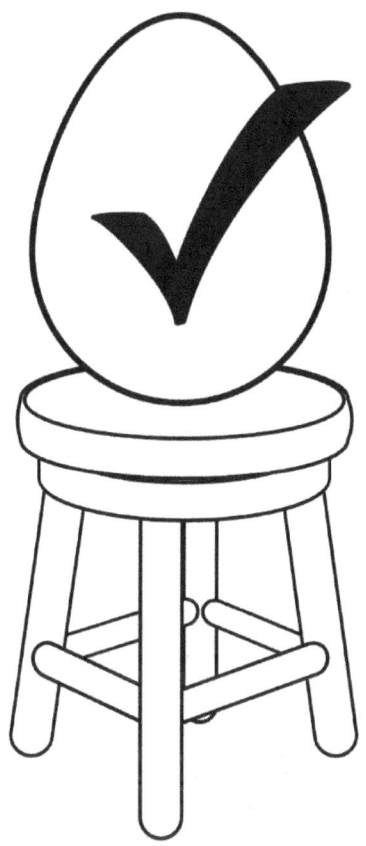

Mastering Commitment

For Software Development Teams

Written by Chris Harden

"Mastering Commitment for Software Development Teams"

Written by Chris Harden

All images and characters are the property of Chris Harden and may not be used without prior written authorization. All characters appearing in this work are anecdotal. Any resemblance to real persons, living or dead is purely coincidental.

©2019, Chris Harden, All Rights Reserved
Published by Peachpi Media

Table of Contents

Table of Contents 3
Before We Begin 4
   Introduction 6
   The Seat: Direction 11
   Leg 1: Resources 23
   Leg 2: Protection 27
   Leg 3: Accountability 37
Leg 4: Motivation 52
   Stain, Paint, Clear Coat: Respect 64
   Fortifiers (Struts) 76
A Side Note: False Fortifiers 111
Commitment: The "Dramper" Formula 113
Shared Staff 125
As a Leader Training Your Culture 131
Stacking and Managing Individuals 134
Wear and Tear 139
When People Put Their Feet Down 145
A Call to Action 148
Tools 150
A Value Template 151
Surveys 153
The Commitment Contract 159
Commitment Contract 161
A Request 162

Dedication 163

Before We Begin

Copies of the Value Statement, Employee Survey, and Commitment Contract in the Tools section of this book are available online. Please visit chrisharden.com/masteringcommitment/supplements to get free copies for your usage.

Introduction

Every successful individual knows that his or her achievement depends on a community of persons working together. -Paul Ryan

Why do we look for commitment from others? Humans are an interdependent species. We rely on others to help us reach our goals. We can do things by ourselves, but we can do so much more when we get others involved to help us reach a goal. A goal is simply an idea with a deadline. Commitment is simply dedicating oneself to meeting that goal.

Entrepreneurs often state ideas are worthless; it is the execution that counts. The bigger your idea, the more you must work to turn that idea into reality. The more work you must do to turn a goal, idea, or target into reality, the more help you need.

Unfortunately, help does not come for free. Not really. We all value time. Therefore, when you want to achieve a goal that requires the help of others, you must provide something in exchange for their commitment to help.

You can inspire people with an idea. You lead them with direction. And you may very well work just as hard as they do to achieve the goal. But in addition to your own individual hard work, your real leadership job involves facilitating their commitment. They will only commit, when you make it possible for them to commit. That's what this book is about – helping you build commitment from individuals, from teams, or as a part of your company culture.

You will learn to use a simple, proven framework to ensure your team meets goals and deadlines. Note that commitment to an ideal, such as "commitment to quality" is more of a general guidance meant to inspire, than it is a clear direction. This book is tactical. It discusses facilitating commitment to concrete goals over clear periods of time. It is not about inspiration; it is about tactical leadership.

I've spent over 20 years in the career path of an engineer, project manager, career manager, corporate executive, and founder. In those 20 years I have worked with many large and small multidisciplinary teams, in a wide variety of industries, such as theme parks, video games, automotive, power, film, consumer products, industrial products, beverages, and mobile devices. My teams have usually been in multiple geographic regions, with portions of them far away from my direct access. I have managed teams on five continents, and I have managed multiple teams on multiple projects at the same time. Those projects have been small, to the tune of $35,000 startups all the way to multi-million dollar projects in Fortune 100 companies. I have learned over the years that no matter what organization I have worked in, teams are teams, and teams always have common problems.

This book is based on a metaphor of an egg sitting on a stool. The egg & stool are a framework that will help you avoid many of the common pitfalls of building commitment, regardless of your context. Teams can have a healthy culture where they last a long time together almost like a family. One of my favorite places I ever worked was in a small company I joined right out of college, and the culture the founder built into his organization resulted in a remarkable level of team health, company commitment, trust, and low turnover. Today, 20 years later, many of my colleagues are still there, love their work, and love the company. They are like a family.

Often, I have also seen the opposite end of the spectrum. Companies can also have a complacent culture, for a variety of reasons. For example, they do not feel respected or heard, they are not committed, and the project direction and completion are just unclear. This normally results in a significant amount of overtime at the end of a milestone, low employee morale, and high attrition, even when the pay is good to great. The ironic part is that large teams may have a ton of resources available to them to get the job done. However, if they don't have other pieces necessary for the team culture to be healthy, no amount of resources in the world can make the team a lasting, efficient, high-quality team with low turnover. In addition, switching to Scrum, Kanban, paired programming, or other Agile development paradigms won't help. Those are all great project management systems that software leaders can apply to drive clarity and capture metrics. But they are not going make a team more successful in reaching deadlines and stepping up when a goal is at risk. What is needed to achieve those goals is a cultural solution.

In this book, I show you a clear metaphor you can share with your teammates to help them to understand their role in the team culture. As a collective, you can avoid some of the major problems most teams experience with bringing a product or service to market year after year. The egg & stool metaphor brings to light all the major pieces necessary to have a strong, trusting team with high commitment and low turnover. It provides a common language you can use to discuss this concept with your teammates, a full team, your manager, or other leaders.

To get started, here is high level summary of the metaphor. Imagine you are trying to balance an egg on a stool. It is possible, but you must be patient and careful to do it. The eggshell represents commitment. The stool represents the infrastructure *you* are creating to help that egg continue to hold its yolk. If you provide a well-built, stable stool for it to rest upon, the egg will continue to sit on top and hold that yolk inside. This is equivalent to someone staying committed to reaching a goal you both set. However, the moment you move the stool, the egg wobbles. Move the stool too much, take away a leg, etc., and you cause the egg to fall off the stool. In doing so, the egg will crack upon hitting the ground, and some or all of the yolk will leak out. It can no longer stay committed to holding the yolk. This is equivalent to that person no longer feeling responsible for reaching your common goal. They try less and rationalize their lack of commitment. If the egg gets only a small crack, you can tape the crack, which is like apologizing or making amends with someone whom you've mistreated, but the crack is still there. You can put the egg back on the stool and ask for further commitment. We all make mistakes, and we can hopefully ask for forgiveness, and try again. But if you *keep* causing the egg to drop and crack further, eventually regardless of the amount of tape you use, the egg simply can't hold the yolk anymore. Any hope of further commitment will be lost.

The first things we explore are all the pieces you need to build the stool, to facilitate commitment. The stool is made of a seat, four legs, and struts. We'll see how each of those key pieces contributes to the whole stool. To facilitate true commitment, you build the whole stool. Without all those pieces in place, you can never expect full commitment from your team. If you can't facilitate commitment, you cannot hold someone accountable. You can certainly try. I have seen managers who do, but they inevitably fail and feel frustrated. Commitment comes from a contract you create between yourself and other individuals. Once you fulfill your part of the contract, you can expect them to fulfill theirs, meaning once you facilitate commitment, you can expect it. Once you build and maintain the right stool, you can honestly expect the egg to rest on top and "hold the yolk."

The Seat: Direction

Men, like nails, lose their usefulness when they lose their direction and begin to bend. - Walter Savage Landor

When you are building a culture there are more pieces to that culture than just the legs of your stool. If I ask you to sketch a stool, you will intuitively also sketch the seat. In fact, it almost seems obvious that a stool must have a seat, otherwise you could not sit upon it. However, many of the metaphors that use stools to describe the key pieces of a solution often fail to discuss the purpose of the seat. Or they label the seat as the overall topic they are trying to explain. However, the seat is one of the five critical pieces of your cultural design. In this metaphor the seat of the stool is the direction that the team is following. If you look at the apex of a stool, the seat is where all four legs connect. This is where they unite for one purpose. *As a leader, it is 100% your responsibility to provide clarity on the goal you are trying to reach. If you are neglecting that responsibility, you are letting your team down.*

Try this exercise sometime. Bring many people together in a room and give them a pencil and a piece of paper. Tell them to do something with the pencil and paper, that they have ten minutes guaranteed without interruption, and that they'll learn something interesting by participating in the exercise. Say nothing more; answer no questions. Leave and return ten minutes later. In doing this, you will have fulfilled their needs for resources, protection, accountability, and motivation. And they will all create something. Or at least most of them will in their own way. Some of them will just write some notes. Some of them will sketch something. Some will crumple or fold the paper. Who knows, some of them might scribble out or erase what they did and try again. Some of them might also speak with each other and unify their efforts. However, as much as they may try, to create something exciting, something that solves a problem for themselves, something that is entertaining, etc. they will end up going in many directions with no unified effort.

* * *

Here is a real-life example. A few years ago, while launching a startup, my business partner and I were invited to an event by one of our biggest community supporters at a local school. The school was for children with special needs, and the event was intended to use the technical community's resources and expertise to solve common problems the students had identified for themselves. The students self-organized a vote for the most important problems that they would like solved. For example, one problem to be solved was playing more easily in a pool with physical disabilities. Another was changing or improving communications devices, so that a person with cerebral palsy could more easily say what they were trying to say. Those are two of about ten problems they identified.

The event organizer invited several of us from the technical community to join the event. We all came to support him not actually understanding what the event was. As the presentation unveiled what we were being asked to do, it became clear to me we were being asked to solve significantly difficult problems in a market space none of us knew anything about. And we were being asked to do so over the span of a couple of weeks. Companies in this industry had not been able to solve these problems in years of research and development. And although that was a concern, we tried to forge ahead anyway.

My business partner and I attended the follow-up meeting of technical contributors, marketers, and product designers. The goal was to pick one or more of the problems, produce a prototype, and eventually build a product that would solve those problems. No one had industry knowledge or was a subject matter expert on how to help children with physical disabilities. So, just like the people in the room with pencil and paper I described earlier, several people made their pitches for immediate ideas, to which two or three others agreed. Some were vocal, and some were reserved or quiet.

We all left the meeting thinking that someone would unify the effort. We assumed someone would pull us altogether and drive the direction for this one unified team. Instead two or three cobbled together teams tried to make progress on two or three half-baked ideas. Two weeks later we were all supposed to come back together with prototypes in hand, and research done. I was part of a chat channel and some email threads and watched what happened.

In the end, one or two individuals had some ideas that they were passionate about, with no one who had the technical savvy necessary or the time available to build those ideas. The resources were not there, not only from a technical savvy standpoint, but a subject matter expert standpoint, and the ability to build these physical prototypes in a time or fashion that made any sense didn't exist. The teams could not rally around a unified direction.

The original invited group included around twenty people. About ten came to the follow-up meeting. The group that carried on a conversation online about five. Only one person tried hard to drive his idea, and no one got behind it. I confess I also did not believe in his idea, because I did not believe we had the resources to execute it. The two-week follow-up meeting we were supposed to have never happened.

I am sure the children were disappointed. I was sad for the children and embarrassed for myself, for everyone else who was asked to attend, and the technical leader who invited us all to the event. Although I understand he was trying his best to start something new and do something great, his failure to fully envision how things would play out and provide a unified direction, set the entire effort up for failure.

The day after the kickoff, he also left the country for a few weeks to manage a different effort, which meant the one person who was most well-positioned to drive the team towards a unified effort was missing. He pulled us all together, and we followed out of respect for him and friendship. He hoped by bringing us together, his effort would turn into something big and drive itself. It did not.

Although I am almost always supportive of trying something out to see how it works and failing fast if it does not, direction must be there. Commitment must be there. And in this case, I was disappointed , because we got all of these children excited, committed to them in some way in their minds, and then neither the team nor the leader delivered.

Years earlier, I consulted for a company in California that made an e-magazine reader. They were growing extremely fast and making money hand over fist. They made one of the first entrances into the e-reader market, grabbed up a lot of market share in the mobile space and were clamoring to stay at the top or close to it. We had a development team working for them on their desktop magazine reader and helping them to redesign it for mobile.

Within a couple of months, we realized the culture there was poisoned. Senior management mistreated the employees and asked them to work insane hours. The management yelled at them and direction changed weekly.

The culture was in a constant management-by-crisis mode. One week these UI changes must be made. The next week there was a security issue and most of the team was put on solving it. Next week there were other architectural issues that came up. On and on it went, and we had our consulting engineers flying down there from Seattle, staying for weeks, and coming back frustrated, worn out and happy they were not working for that company full-time. We also lost two members of our consulting company who had burned out and did not want to work for that customer anymore.

Consistent direction did not exist. The culture was not unified. And it led to attrition and a complete lack of trust.

* * *

Every time you change the direction of your team, it is like you are spinning or removing the seat on their stool. In the egg & stool metaphor, the seat is a swivel seat. It can be rotated back and forth, so you can gently tweak your direction here and there, and still save commitment. But if you are rapidly and frequently switching directions or changing direction in a big way the egg can't stay balanced, and it falls. Commitment is broken, and you need to rebuild it. In terms of people, you risk taking away all the trust you have built by asking them to stand while you swap out the seat (completely change directions or "pivot"). When they stand, they can just as easily choose to walk away as they can to sit back down.

* * *

I have also worked on teams where the direction was clear and consistent. These teams had good leadership in place, and the leadership was willing to make decisions and cut features as needed to keep us on task.

Upon joining a 15-person game development team, my co-manager and I immediately noticed the team had a lot of problems. The biggest problem was the UI tool other game teams needed from us was completely unusable. They had to build all their user interfaces with code instead of a user-friendly, drag and drop tool.

We set a clear goal for our team: overhaul the layout tool so that other game teams could use it for intuitive user interface designs.

We set a clear very clear timeline: get it done within 2.5 months. We told the team to do nothing but this overhaul. Everyone was on board, because we explained what was at stake for the team. I think they were excited to finally have the focus be so clear. All hands were on deck and for the next two and a half months, they did nothing but rebuild the tool. It was intense and we worked a lot of overtime, but the team nailed it. In the end the tool was awesome, and it was usable by the game dev teams. We also gave frequent deployments to the customer teams. They gave us feedback and the direction stayed laser focused on the end goal of having very specific, customer-requested features usable end to end by those teams.

Direction was easier to define at the outset when I launched a small software startup called TROBO. TROBO was a plush toy connected to a storytelling mobile app. I acted as the Product Owner in addition to the Scrum master or project manager and early system architect. Like is often done in startups, I wore many hats, which made direction simpler. As the Product Owner, I identified the business features the product would support. On the creative side, I drove development of the production scripts writers created, designed the interactive puzzles in the stories, directed the art our team built for avatars and backgrounds, and produced the entirety of the story. As the technical director, I provided direction to the engineering team on how things should be built. As a Product Owner, I had to make tough choices on features we would support and what features were out of scope (i.e. unaffordable in the timeframe we had left to get to market).

TROBO had a much smaller team; I hired three engineers, four artists, and four writers. With a small number of stakeholders in the conversation, and clarity on where we knew we had to be to reach a minimum shippable product, it was easy to keep the direction of the team clear, and we progressed in a timely fashion and got to market.

The team was empowered on the engineering side to make their own decisions under the hood, as long as they followed good engineering practices such as code reviews, documentation, source control, and good object-oriented design. The content team was encouraged to make their own decisions regarding color palettes for stories and character designs if they adhered to production guidelines (such as script reviews and storyboards) and followed style guides.

Both teams worked in a project management tool called JIRA and they saved and shared their art and their code with SVN. The teams' expectations were set right from the beginning on what they should own, according to the things I cared about as a technical director, art director, and producer for the product. As teams get larger it is harder to ensure consistent direction from upper management is clearly communicated to everyone on the team. With a small team it is much easier to communicate.

* * *

As individual contributors (non-managers) become more senior in their roles, they are able to see the leadership needs more clearly. Things make sense to them, because they know the technology or the product so well from years past. Consistent direction communicated from leadership and from senior members on the team to junior members on the team is one of the key things needed to make the stool stable for that team. It is what is needed to make a stable culture for a team. If you have highly talented, trained, or motivated teammates being redirected every few weeks to build something new, cancel half-built features, or redo work they just completed a few weeks earlier (called "churn"), no matter how highly skilled or passionate they are, they will get demotivated. They will feel mistreated. They will get frustrated. They will get distracted. And they will be less effective at their jobs.

The direction changes can come all the way from the CEO, from VPs, from marketing directors, from Product Owners or feature owners, or from designers on the team itself. If the team often receives changing designs or direction, you essentially have a wobbly stool. Providing strong and clear direction that does not waver over time will keep your team feeling in-charge, minimize frustration, and minimize attrition. They will feel like the company cares about them and the hard work they are investing to move forward. Yes, things will change from time to time. Yes, adapting to those changes is what it means to be agile. But large directional changes must be carefully managed. I once saw a huge team that lost a year's worth of development time, because the CEO's reaction during a review was miscommunicated through management and affected the entire team for months before the miscommunication was detected.

Changing directions frequently has a major impact on any team. The morale gets hurt. The culture gets hurt. And talented people leave.

* * *

What does this mean for you as a leader? What does it mean for you as an individual on a team with leaders? It means try to cultivate a culture where major changes are thoroughly considered instead of being made on a whim. Where the direction being set up front for a team is discussed as fully as possible with as many stakeholders as possible and is clearly agreed-upon by the stakeholders before being communicated out.

Amazon has a culture of "agree or disagree and then execute". This means even if you don't agree, once you align on a direction, have the integrity to support that direction. I agree with that. I once met an engineering director for a casino gaming company who told me as a test of engineering etiquette (and I think team etiquette in general), he interviewed people to ensure they would be willing to agree to disagree, but then still execute.

I have seen politics be very distracting in organizations, where people did not agree, and then they went off to their own tribes and tried to escalate up their own chains to get the direction for the team or a feature reshaped according to how they saw fit. When you see a situation like that developing in meetings where people do not agree, see if you can surface that and be honest. You can ask the team, "I understand we are disagreeing here, but how can we agree to disagree but still execute?" Ask people if they will support the direction that is chosen. Ask leaders to discuss the impact when they change the direction three weeks from now. "What will happen if we change this feature in three weeks? Will it demoralize the team? Is changing this direction later or behind the scenes really the best decision?"

Often, people are so focused on getting something *they* want out of a situation they do not think about how it affects the overall project or team. In the end, you want that team to be there year after year, and one minor feature will not make a difference. So, help leaders to understand changing things without care can have significant impacts.

In summary, identify and communicate the target clearly. Get commitment to reach it. Provide clear and unwavering direction on how you want to accomplish the goal through the period. If you are doing these things, you are doing one piece of *your* job to drive *their* commitment.

Leg 1: Resources

A lack of resources may slow you down, but don't let it make you throw away a big idea. - Robert H. Schuller

Resources are usually not a problem for large companies. They are often a problem for startups or small businesses with jagged sales cycles or cash flows. Resources, or a severe lack of them, are probably the most obvious things anyone on the team will recognize. Resources in this case are computers, software, standard office supplies, telephones, backend IT, security, office space, travel, copiers, printers, kitchen areas, restrooms, parking, other infrastructure, and, frankly, people.

Although we take those things for granted in a large company, it can be a problem for those at the opposite end of the spectrum. Startups just don't have the same easy access to resources as multibillion-dollar corporations. I have been in the startup world, and picking the right office space that is cheap, doesn't have expensive parking, has access to many of the things listed above, and is reachable by the team members, is not a trivial thing.

Community is also important. In startups, the community is outward. It's in your neighborhood. It's in your city, and it may be virtual. Co-working in an open space can be powerful when launching a company. It can lead to meeting (or networking with) people in your community to back and support you. More importantly, your community can help fortify you, because you simply don't have the money as a startup.

Community for a large organization is more inward. You can look to the different office locations or a different team in your company for help. Large companies generally have all the necessary infrastructure (or at least most of it). Normally, resources are less of a concern for large organizations, but they can become a larger concern for very small teams within the organization. For example, when you are an intrapreneur (an employee who promotes innovation within the limits of his/her organization), you may often be cash restrained. You may not have much budget to hire the teammates you need to do to deliver on your grand idea or research and development project.

When it comes to resources, it is easy to overlook the basics and how those missing pieces can put your team *culture* at risk. For example, let's say you have joined a team that has been around for a while, but all of their equipment is old. Or the team is mature, but you're headed into new territory, and the team does not have the skills or expertise necessary to solve the problem. In the first case, you are faced with spending your money on buying new computers, so your team can stay up-to-date and move quickly. If you don't, you're putting them at risk of being demotivated, because your tools are slowing them down. In the second case, if you are taking your team into new learning territory, some of them might be quite excited to learn something new. In fact, most people will be excited to learn something new, if they believe it will help them in their long-term career. However, if you're taking your team in a direction the members don't want to go, that will start to damage your team culture. The team members may no longer trust where you are headed, and they will start looking for other opportunities.

For managers, changing resources and maintaining resources is something you must handle in the long term. With the egg & stool metaphor, if you envision resources as one of the legs, imagine what happens if you don't have as many resources as you need to do the job. The stool will tilt or fall. Go ahead and document the resources you will need and confirm them with your team.

If you are an employee being asked to deliver on a piece of work, but you are struggling, do a sanity check to ensure you have the right resources you need. If you don't, ask for them and be prepared to explain how having them will improve your performance.

The most common way to cause an effort to fail is to restrain the resources it needs to fulfill the commitment. This can happen where you are told you'll have the resources you'll need, but when you get started, or during the process, it becomes a struggle to get or keep those resources. If you see this occurring, have an earnest conversation with your upper management to get the resources retained, back in place, etc. or ask to revisit the original commitment, since the elements leading to that original commitment have changed.

If your teammates see resources being taken away, they will also need to see what you are doing to protect the resources you have left. Seeing this will help them maintain their commitment.

Leg 2: Protection

Chekov: "Shields up, Captain?"

Valeris: "Captain, our shields!"

Chekov: "Shields up, Captain?"

- "Star Trek VI: The Undiscovered Country", Star date 9523.8

I often regard the work I have done when protecting my team as "raising shields". When time comes to protect your team, perhaps envisioning yourself as a Captain raising the shields will inspire you as it has me. If you are not a Star Trek fan, pick your own heroic situation where you are gallantly protecting your team. Protection is the next leg in a strongly built stool.

Protection failures can occur when managers allow salespeople, marketing teams, Product Owners, business owners, or other leaders in general, to change requirements during development cycles. Without protection from leaders, individual commitment stops. We'll discuss that leg in the next chapter, but it's important to realize the consequences poor protection can cause.

Protection for a development team simply means allowing them to do their job without confusion or distraction during a set period. In an ideal world, where requirements don't change, protection is easy. At the beginning of a period where you are creating a product, you would simply say, "build the product with these features", and the development team would go do that. They would return in two or three weeks with an additional set of features for you to review. And those features would be perfect. Of course, the world is not ideal. We cannot simply say, "build these features", and have the development team successfully create them in a vacuum, nor can they do it perfectly every time.

There is a management process called Waterfall management. Waterfall management does in fact follow a similar pattern, where the features are designed up front and agreed-upon. Then the development team creates the product or features and then returns with the completed product. That is true at least to a small degree. It used to be the way many things were built. In fact, manufacturing still runs this way, which is appropriate. At least it is for mass manufacturing when you want to build many of the same widget. In this scenario, the design has already been completed, and the production team is simply replicating it as quickly as they can while getting the best quality that they can, on budget. Waterfall works well in a manufacturing scenario. And until about 15 years to 20 years ago, software development teams were run in the same way. And large, fixed-price military contracts, are still done this way to a degree. A company will hire a contracting company to build something. They agree upon the price and features, and development is started. There is oversight to ensure that development team is correctly building the product to spec. And supposedly at the end of the development, the customer has a working product according to specs. But again around 15 to 20 years ago, software development companies recognized this was the wrong way to build software with a value to end customers. That's because we don't always understand what our customer needs when we start a project. We and they don't have clairvoyance. So, instead the community created agile development methodologies. If you are a software developer, you take this for granted these days. But if you are not, here is a brief description.

There is someone who understands the business value of what the software development team must create. That someone is called a "Product Owner" or a "Feature Owner". The team is responsible for turning a feature set into a working software product or physical product that has features such as a toy, an Internet of Things (IoT) device like a Bluetooth connected home device, or cars as an example. The amount of quick iteration that is done on products that are mass manufactured will have a lot of iteration while in the research and development (R&D) phases. Then once the design has been ironed out, the company will go into a waterfall manufacturing scenario. In the world of software, because you do not invest a large amount of upfront capital to "mass manufacture" your software on an assembly line, your teams can continue to iterate either daily, weekly, monthly, quarterly, or annually and so on. Agile methodology is where you constantly assess how the customer works with your product and where they find value. Doing so allows the development teams to iterate quickly. That is a real benefit of agile development and modern software techniques.

However, there is also a huge risk inherent in agile development methodologies. *The risk in agile development is introduced when the software development team cannot control itself.* That risk occurs when the Product Owner, business owner feature owner, CEO, VP of product development, or marketing team gets into the habit of changing requirements so quickly that they randomize the development team's ability to work on anything consistently.

The most common example is the scenario where a development team has no defined development period, such as two or three weeks. They just develop on the whims of the CEO, VP of development, or the Producer of the product. For example, one week into developing the next feature set, the Product Owner comes in and asks a developer or two to do something "really quick." It shouldn't take long right?

The nice developer who just wants to help and who appreciates the opportunity to prove their worth says yes and goes on to develop a new, shiny feature instead of the one he or she committed to at the beginning of the development period. When this happens, the person has essentially decided the new and shiny feature is more important than the feature they committed to in the previous week.

Often, the CEO, VP of development, or marketing representative assume that not only will the original features get done, but even the new asks will also get done, and it will all come in on time at the end of the development period. They think that by asking for it "on the side," the developers can work magic and get it all done. They don't realize any questions or requests that come in after the team has started will have an impact on the development schedule. That problem is so common in software development, it is one of the main reasons why agile methodologies were created.

Almost every software development group you run into today is using some sort of agile methodology, and many of them use Scrum. *Or so they say they do.*

I have been on many teams that think they use Scrum, but instead they don't fully understand it or the end goal. I have lost count of how many times this falsehood has occurred. The problem I am describing is this:

A team is trying to use Scrum. They commit to two to four weeks of development. They have a planning meeting at the beginning of that time and decide they are going to develop seven features. Two weeks in, the business representative comes in and asks for something different. The business representative will ask one developer to do something which is not in the feature set. Then another business representative will come in and ask a different developer for help on something else. Maybe they have design questions for the next period. Or maybe they have a business meeting on Monday, and they really need some help preparing a demo. The demo promises to change the world, if the salesperson can land the deal.

There are many justifiable reasons why outside stakeholders will ask the development team to do something else and get distracted from their goal for that development cycle. The developers will kindly attempt to absorb all these outside requests. The management staff on the development team don't even know the requests are coming in. The requests are not surfaced in a daily meeting (if there is one). The staff don't tell the managers these requests are being made. It is not until the end of the sprint the development team realizes it has missed its goals.

Ironically, the developers cannot even explain what happened. They did not realize they were sacrificing their goals set forth at the beginning of the development in order to help with all these unplanned, outside requests.

At the end of the development, four of the seven features have been created. People work extra hours. Then the Product Owners ask, "Why wasn't everything completed?"

No one knows. All the little fires that were requested throughout the development have been forgotten. Most weren't documented in the first place. The sales call happened, and the salesperson did not land the deal. The marketing demo happened, but so what? And the CEO's new whiz-bang feature that was the hottest thing on Wednesday last week is no longer of interest.

Everyone has moved on to the next fire, the next whiz-bang request, the next sale, the next demo.

Randomization has happened many times, and the development team cannot explain what happened. This goes on for months or even years until finally someone recognizes this cultural problem. This all circles around one word: protection. Protection is the leg of the stool I have most often seen missing on teams I have been a part of. Protection of the team is absolutely the most challenging service leaders must provide.

In order to protect your team, you must start with "no". You must start with "please wait". You must start with, "Hey, that sounds like a great idea. We will put it in our backlog and revisit it at the end of this development cycle. " You must tell people their need for immediate satisfaction must wait.

You must tell that sales representative, "I'm sorry you just cannot use this developer to create your demo on Tuesday. You must come up with something else to solve that problem. "

You must tell the marketing VP that they cannot get the assistance to put out a new fire, create a new demo, or create a new mockup for Sunday. You must say, "I'm sorry, but we had already committed to this amount of work so that the product can ship next month."

You must be what they will perceive as the bad guy. And that is the easy part. In order to truly protect your team, you must *train your team to protect itself.*

For example, as a leader, you will start training your team to refrain from accepting outside requests. Designers, Product Owners, even the vice president of marketing or the CEO will still come to your team and ask for favors or a quick solution. You *must* tell the team they *cannot* do those favors.

You can offer yourself as a protective wall. You can empower them by teaching them to say, "My manager has told me I cannot do any outside work, so please talk with him/her first." This is especially helpful with junior contributors.

Junior contributors do not know they are getting into this trouble. They do not know they're allowing themselves to be distracted by a well-intentioned business owner or Product Owner or feature owner. They're just being nice, albeit naive. Anyone who is a senior to them in the organization feels like a boss asking them to do something. They want to please their boss. They want to do a good job. By telling them to redirect everyone who asks for something back to you, you at least help to calm the noise.

For your more senior people, it can be more of an issue to get them to honor your request to stay focused. They are senior. They have opinions. They might very well agree this new whiz-bang feature requested by someone else *is* more important than the features you committed to at the beginning of the cycle. When this happens, they are inherently, and perhaps quite consciously, undermining the plan of the team during that development period. If they do not agree the team needs protection, or they do not agree they themselves need protection, then you have a much harder task. It means it will have to be more of a sales effort on your part to convince your senior developers to support your overall plan.

As a leader you must manage upward and outward to protect your team. To use the Star Trek paradigm, you must raise your shields around the team. In terms of Scrum, the Scrum Master must protect the team. If you are not a manager, then read these next paragraphs knowing your team is just as accountable as the manager is.

The team's ability to deliver reliably will struggle, if the team is not also protecting itself. It usually takes 2 to 4 development cycles for a team to understand the idea and impact of protecting itself. If a team is not protected by its leadership, it will never complete the features it committed to at the beginning of the development period. If individuals do not protect themselves from outside asks, the team will never finish all the features it committed to.

Protection is absolutely the hardest leg to put on the stool *and* keep there. Everyone in the organization must understand and support protection. If they don't, the team will never make its deadlines. It will fail every single time.

It is also your responsibility to protect the team from your own leadership mistakes. A common mistake I have observed is inadvertently taking away your team's autonomy. Here's how it usually goes: You have the team come into a planning meeting. You have pre-assigned all their tasks. You've provided the estimates or asked a lead to provide all the estimates because "leads clearly know how to estimate work." You tell them to get started. At the end of the cycle you hold them accountable for delivery on the features that you gave them and all the estimates that someone else made. This is an easy mistake to make because it is only a slight twist on the Scrum paradigm. However, in this scenario you have taken away all autonomy. As a result, you have damaged or completely obliterated their protection from you, their leader. Then, as a result, when you try to hold them accountable for this work, they can simply say, "I tried my best, but you gave me too much work" or "I tried my best, but those estimates were wrong. I did not estimate them" or "I tried my best, but I was not in control of the situation."

In the end, protection is so critical to a team's success that without it, you might as will not have a team. Just don't make the mistake of attempting to hold the team accountable when you have not given them the tools to control their own destiny. Resources, which is leg one and protection, which is leg two, when combined enable you generate commitment. Providing a measure of accountability is a way of checking on that commitment. If you haven't noticed yet, all of these legs work together. You cannot have one without the others. Your stool cannot stand on one leg or two legs. You must have at least three legs for the stool to be somewhat usable, and there is a very important fourth, stabilizing leg. We'll get to leg three, accountability, next.

Leg 3: Accountability

"A body of men holding themselves accountable to nobody ought not to be trusted by anybody." –Thomas Paine

The quote above may seem to start off this chapter a bit negatively, however it really drives home a key message. You're reading this to learn how to build trust in an organization. Without a doubt, if your team or company does not hold itself accountable, it cannot be trusted. The opposite holds true as well. If your team holds itself accountable, it is inherently more trustworthy.

The third leg of our metaphor of a committed culture is accountability. Accountability simply means delivering the work you committed to deliver with an acceptable or higher level of quality, on time, and on budget. The key to accountability taking measurements. *Whether you are measuring yourself or someone or some mechanism is providing the service, measurement is how you ensure accountability.*

When a team comes together to accomplish a common goal, they must agree on the resources they are using to get to that goal, what that goal is, and what their "definition of done" looks like. If they don't agree at the beginning on the resources, the goal itself, and what "done" means, they will have misaligned expectations. When expectations are not aligned properly, someone will believe someone else on the team has failed or that the team has entirely failed.

Note that accountability, as I am discussing it in this book, is not simply an internal, honorable approach to life. The way accountability is driven is by measuring deliverables. If a team is actively measuring itself against whether it meets its commitments or not, the team will meet them more often. Accountability in this chapter is about having active, regular accountability *measures* that are openly shared with all stakeholders.

Not all measures are quantitative. Although I think Key Performance Indicators (KPIs) can provide good value, I'll give you an action you can take and an example of an accountability measure that is qualitative in nature. The first thing you will do is over communicate with the group and with individuals that you will increasingly begin holding them accountable for their estimates and commitments. In your career mentoring "one-on-ones", explain your expectations. If they are junior members tell them they must review the estimates with someone who is more senior. Tell them you understand that they will not get their estimates perfect. However, they are expected to review their estimates with someone who can confirm or educate their estimates. Also tell the Leads that they are responsible for the quality of the junior peoples' estimates on their team. In the team meetings, when you are all coming together to review what will be done in the next development cycle, you tell them they have "homework". You explain that by the commitment meeting, which will happen a day later, that they should have had all the meetings they need to and have broken down their tasks into estimates. They should be able to come in that morning and commit to deliver on the tasks that they are signed up for. Understand they must sign up for the tasks. They must be able to choose and assign the task to themselves as individuals. You give them a list of features that you want done in the period. You ask them to assess which and how much they can do. You let them commit. Then you remove the features that cannot be done or were not signed up for by anyone. Then you tell them, "Great job on signing up for this, now are you ready to commit to delivering it at the end of the development cycle."

If people come into the commitment meeting without having broken down their tasks, that is a clear and measurable request. Ask them to explain why. Let silence be your friend. Ask them and then be quiet. After a while of doing this, they will feel more obligated to get their "homework" done on time. This subtlety is important. The first development cycle will not be perfect. People will not have their estimates done correctly, and they will not meet their commitments.

That's okay. You are changing a culture over time. But over two or three cycles, you will see a change. You'll give them feedback in their one-on-ones to let them know they are doing well, or they need to do better. You will then hold them accountable in front of the team for good estimates and commitments to deliver. What you want to see is that they feel obligated to the team to deliver. They should not only feel obligated to you. The more they feel obligated to the team, the more they will deliver to the team. *Your goal shall be that they care more about what the team needs than they do about what you think.* This way if you leave, the team's successful habits will stay intact.

As I mentioned before, if you are going to expect the team to be accountable, you must protect their ability to be accountable. You protect them by stopping stakeholders who ask for unplanned favors during the development period, and you give them autonomy in making their own decisions in breaking down their work and choosing tasks from a pool of the most important features. If you get the sense that someone does not understand what you were doing, it is your responsibility to re-frame the message. Some people comprehend messaging better from emails, some people comprehend better from conversations like one-on-ones, and some people comprehend better from meetings. That is why you must communicate in multiple ways. And repeat yourself. It is OKAY to repeat yourself. I often remind myself that in any given meeting of 10 people, at least one person is always distracted. If you respect the fact that our minds wander, perhaps because we have life getting in the way, and we might just not hear what you had to say, then your message is worth repeating. I had an instance where I communicated a specific deadline in both a meeting and via email. And several of my lead people were off by a week in their understanding of that deadline. They were surprised. In that scenario I just pointed them back to the email that had the correct date. So, in addition to verbally communicating it and documenting it in an email, I still missed communicating this deadline to a point where they got it clearly. Was it my fault? Was it theirs? It was both of ours. Communication is always a two-party responsibility. On many of the teams I have managed, especially the ones that were in trouble when I joined, commitment was simply not a part of the culture. Pieces of commitment were there. Unfortunately, without all the pieces in place, regardless of how well-intended individuals are in keeping themselves accountable or in keeping a team accountable, if everyone on the team is not setting the right standard of expectations on accountability by measuring the delivery on commitments, most of the team will fail to be accountable. If the team is not holding its individuals accountable, commitments will continue to be missed.

On one very large team I joined midway in my career, I saw a lack of accountability almost across the board. The organization was roughly 200 people. It was a one-year development cycle, and it was made up of multiple disciplines: engineers, user interface developers, artists, designers, producers, management, quality assurance, etc... The team was made up of several sub teams. When I joined, I noticed, even at the individual level, people were not acting as a team.

The sub-disciplines were not self-coordinating and self-leveling their workloads. Individuals would run out of work to do and not ask for more. Others had too much to finish and worked overtime. Some would not identify dependencies on their work for teammates or vice versa, which would result in some team members getting blocked halfway through the development effort.

We had three-week development periods call sprints. In general, the team did not consider it a priority to deliver all of the features they had intended to deliver. It was considered "no big deal" if you had five features to deliver by the end of the sprint and you only delivered four. The fifth one was called "overhang," and almost everyone had it. The result of overhang in a software development project, is that features initially planned to be developed in the product don't get done. They may never get done and completely get left on the cutting room floor. Product Owners struggle to keep as much of their features in their product as they can, especially when they have a deadline they must meet. In our case we had an annually shipping product, so we had to cut features as the deadline got closer.

Most of this was happening, because none of the teams in that particular organization did any reviews of their work. No one's progress was being measured. They had overhang at the end of each development period. They were not communicating well. They did not know where their dependencies were. All of this resulted in them continuing to slide feature after feature, later and later. Features were cut, and the Product Owner got less of the product they wanted. Had the communications and tracking been strong on the front end, and had people been willing to commit to delivering on their commitments, more features and more business value could have been delivered to the customer when the product shipped.

Early on, I was able to win the support of my fellow leaders on the team to add those checkpoints back in. The team already knew about these checkpoints, but it had just fallen into neglectful ways due to schedule pressures, feature churn, and lots of other organization-wide cultural problems.

Over the next several sprints I worked with them to add pieces of culture around accountability measures. The missing checkpoints were the standard sprint demonstrations and reviews where you look at what you did well, look at what you did poorly, and discuss what you can do better the next time. Our demonstrations allowed the team to show the features that they had completed, and more importantly, allow them to see what features were really not "DONE" done, even though the team said they were. There is something quite powerful about showing your work to the rest of the team and/or outside stakeholders that helps your team to shore up the quality level on what they *say* is done versus what they *assume* is done. Doing this also helps confirm end to end functionality as opposed to just one of the disciplines getting their job done while the others failed to do so.

I believe people are fundamentally driven to do the right thing. This check and balance is not about assuming the worst in people and then acting as "big brother" to ensure they do the job. This approach is quite contrary to that concept. Instead what I believe is that people let their assumptions get the best of them. They assume it will all just work together, if they get their part done. They assume that by having created something, it will just work when needed. However, time and time again, I have seen demos fail. The demos force assumptions to be tested in the realm of reality. End to end accountability checking is extremely important when you are trying to ship a product or service. But where all of this starts is with each individual's understanding the expectations of accountability.

It turned out many people were quite excited to see the checkpoints put back into the process. A key part of my success re-implementing them was that the other leaders supported my efforts. If you do not have "buy in" from your leaders to help affect cultural change, it will be a struggle, if not an eventual failure.

* * *

Please know that if you are familiar with Scrum, the scenario above where teams are skipping demos, is a perfect example of a team who follows part of the mechanics of Scrum, but in reality the culture of the team is failing to understand the real value in actually adhering to the guidance. You can say you are doing Scrum, but the proof around whether the team is following through is in the cultural pudding. Skipping demos is skipping an accountability measure. Don't. skip. demos.

* * *

Two or three sprints in, I discussed with the team the concept of completing your workload and asking for more as opposed to having your manager tell you what you'll do next. Basically, I trained the individuals to understand they were expected to own their discipline. Once the individuals began to understand they were expected to own their delivery, and they were expected to own getting more work instead of being told what to do, they were quite empowered. You could see a sense of independence with the individuals and a sense of stronger teamwork as each discipline figured out how to self-balance its workload. Instead of one person working overtime to catch up and another person getting to go home early, because he finished all of his commitments, the sub team would have a meeting halfway through the development cycle and re-level the workload so that the *team* finished together and had roughly the same amount of work throughout the period. It wasn't perfect mind you, but it was a lot better than it had been before. The team felt stronger, because they could self-coordinate. Self-coordination is a key part of accountability. In the end, in the unlikely event I was not able to attend a sprint demo, the team knew what to do. *It did not need me to hold it accountable. It was holding itself accountable.* When you have accomplished this with your team, congratulations, you now have a real leg of accountability.

* * *

Another part of a team's accountability is one around engagement of Quality Assurance (QA). I have joined teams (and just seen teams on the periphery) that don't fully value the addition that quality assurance brings to their work. Even in some of the most mature organizations, I have seen quality assurance underrepresented.

Several years ago, I joined a team that managed user interface technology. This team was made up of roughly 15 engineers and a technical artist. I took over this team along with a co-manager. This team was in trouble, because they were not delivering on promises made to C-level management two years earlier.

Along with the obvious issues, the team had sorely under used quality assurance. And even though they were part of a huge, multibillion-dollar company, the use of quality assurance had not really occurred to them. They had one QA representative do some tests a few hours per week, "as needed." Again, this was a team of 15 people creating all sorts of wonderful features. They were following some aspects of agile software development. They had good resources (PCs, software, etc.). For many of the aspects of their cultural stool, they were doing OKAY. However, accountability was absolutely a short leg.

Just having a part-time quality assurance person to handle everything 15 people could build was clearly a mismatch of resources. My immediate action was to begin conversations with my boss and ask him where we could find the money for quality assurance to join us and begin filing bugs, doing testing of the new features, checking the old ones, etc.

Within a month and a half, we had regular quality insurance coverage by one lead QA person and two others in training. They were also ramping up a team at our remote center that did a lot of standard testing for the company. This third-party oversight of the work was able to help the team keep their quality high and to track their delivery commitments. They were able to more clearly articulate what was going to be delivered at the end of the development, because the quality assurance team was now expecting these features and writing tests for the features.

Before my co-manager and I joined the team, this team was not holding itself accountable for what the company was *paying it to build*. Therefore, without clear goals that would then be vetted by QA partners, the team floundered. Having QA vet their work forced the team to reach a sense of clarity.

By the way, my co-manager saw the same need for QA, and we were in immediate agreement on what to do. That's another example of the value in having leadership "buy in" to support your cultural changes.

When a team does not have the money to pay for quality assurance, that indicates a resourcing problem. Mainly, the money has been all spent towards development and no money has been spent towards the QA. It is sometimes hard to pay for QA if you are struggling to get a business unit off the ground. However, it is important to remember that quality assurance is a long-term protective solution that increases the quality of your product.

If you cannot find the money to add individual QA members or outsourced QA solutions to your team, the next best step is to build the quality assurance time into your own developers' schedules. Force them to do quality-control on their own code by simply having one engineer quality control another engineer's work. By having someone else perform user testing on your code, or feature testing on your work, they will begin to see problems that you assumed did not exist as an engineer. This technique is sometimes called "eating your own dog food." By having a small team eat their own dog food and ensure the quality control is high, you can still ensure that some basic quality checks are being performed. In this case you will educate your development staff on the value of finding their own bugs.

Here's how you can do it. Have your team do a "release cycle", which was essentially a development cycle just before your next release. Take the first week and do nothing but try to find bugs and document them. Then have most of the team fix the bugs until they run out, and then they can come back and perform more quality assurance. They should identify high, medium, and low impact bugs, and then you can instruct them on which ones are critically needed to be addressed and which ones you are willing to let go until later. Cosmetic bugs are often allowed to go to later cycles, because in the early days of the cycle, you'll probably have many critical level bugs to address.

This is a form of accountability you can accomplish without having to bring on a formal QA team, and it works great in startups or on teams in companies that don't yet have QA teams established to help. Sometimes you need time to hire a team, but you can still "eat your own dog food" while you wait to get formal QA in place.

Another thing to consider in accountability is how much autonomy you are providing. On one of my teams, many of the engineers would wait until a manager would tell them the work to do next, as I mentioned earlier. Your engineers are professionals. Your artists are professionals. Your teammates are professionals. They are paid to do the work. They are paid to know the needs of the product. *If you must tell your teammates what to do all the time, you and they have shifted the accountability for their work onto you.* When your team holds itself accountable, you can focus more on the right things such as setting direction, providing resources, protecting the team, and maintaining team culture. If you are forced to tell them what to do every day, you are stuck in the day-to-day mire of a bad management situation.

    For managers, over the next few weeks, watch for opportunities to help your team increase their level of accountability. If you see an individual who is not owning the delivery of her work, have a one-on-one with that teammate and explain the value of doing that. Explain that when you are not in her way, she can move more quickly and add more value for the customer. She will be more in control of her career, and people will notice. There are always ways to motivate people to increase their sense of ownership. You just must find the ones that work for your members. And if it is a team wide cultural issue, consider creating a presentation that discusses ownership. The presentation will discuss how valuable it is for them to self-coordinate. This will help them to maintain the speed of delivery that they should as a team, while keeping the quality high. Show them how as a manager you should not be a bottleneck in their communications, because it will only slow them down. If you are concerned removing yourself from the middle of their communications will somehow devalue your work as a manager, take heart. By removing yourself as the bottleneck between your development members when they are trying to self-coordinate their work, you allow yourself to fly a little higher above the team and see other problems you can help solve. That is one difference between management and leadership. Managers will get stuck in the day-to-day grind of trying to keep up and ensuring everyone has work. Leaders will encourage those individuals to act as "companies of one" driving their individual careers and driving the team's success as a player on that team. Leaders will facilitate self-direction. They will facilitate accountability, and in exchange for their freed-up time, the leaders can go on to solve other cultural issues on the team. If we revisit our metaphor, by allowing the team to focus on the accountability leg, you will be able to focus on the direction of the team.

For individuals, much of what I just described above applies to you too. If you want to make a change in your team's level of accountability, the only different recommendation I will make to you is that you watch the team in the same ways above, but then raise the suggestions to your manager or to your team during your sprint reviews. I recommend you do it during your reviews with a set of positively directed questions. For example, "Do you guys think it would be wise of us to get some better end to end demos going just to ensure this is all plugging together well?" If you get a sense some suggestion or request may seem like you are trying to take over your manager's job, then considering offering that one up for discussion with your manager before you share it with the team. That may be a more effective way to achieve the goal, until you know your manager trusts your suggestions for the team. The key to successfully building this leg is 1. Agreeing up on clear measurements of success, 2. Communicating when you'll measure, 3. Measuring and discussing the results in a recurring, frequent pattern.

Leg 4: Motivation

"Of course, motivation is not permanent. But then, neither is bathing; but it is something you should do on a regular basis."
- Zig Ziglar, Raising Positive Kids in a Negative World

Why will people will do things when they don't have enough resources, when they are not necessarily as protected as they could be from outside interference, or despite the fact they're not necessarily being held accountable with a measure of some sort? Why will people stay at a job they don't like? Why will entrepreneurs attempt the impossible journey of starting a company from scratch, build it with no income for years, and put their family finances at real risk? Why will some people on your team work twice or three times the number of hours of the rest of your team members? Some people may do something despite all odds, for reasons that are not obvious to you on the surface. Regardless of whether you can identify the reasons or not, they all add up to motivation, the fourth leg in the stool. And, when you can't seem to get someone to do something, no matter what you try, motivation is also where you can look.

I admit my initial draft of this book and cultural model had three legs - resources, protection, and accountability measures. After working with the three-legged model for a couple years and seeing a mix of the situations I just described in the intro to this chapter, I realized I was missing something. That fourth aspect, motivation, is multidimensional and perhaps the most complicated piece of the stool.

Since my time as a sales rep with The Southwestern Company, I have been listening to Zig Ziglar, one of the most successful motivational speakers in history. His quote above charmingly reminds us to work at *motivating* our teams. However first, I want to discuss motivation a bit differently here. I want to discuss regularly *gauging* the motivation of your team members to learn whether their motivation naturally aligns with where your team is headed. It quite frankly may not be, or it may change, but your job here is to watch your team and ultimately know what things are motivating everyone. You'll do this, so you can guide your team, mitigate risks if someone is indicating they are distracted or not bought in to the direction, make corrections when you can, or even plan for their departure, which you may have no control over. Since you cannot control all the things that motivate people, you must work to influence the ones you can, discover the ones you can't, and plan as best you can to adapt when they affect your people's decisions.

Also, in times of personal unhappiness, where you may be feeling like you don't belong with a program or a company, you can look at it through this lens. You may recognize that your personal motivations have changed, the direction the team, project, or company has taken have changed, or for some other reason, your personal motivations are no longer aligned with the direction of the effort. Or you may just reconfirm that you are aligned, yet you are in a short period where things are just tough at the moment. You can then determine whether you want to actively work to realign your motivations or to part ways. By looking through this lens of the motivation leg, you can do so from a clear perspective instead of just using a gut feeling.

The easiest example of someone who has strong motivation is anyone that you have come across who tends to have "drive". When people look at that person and they say, "wow, he is driven", or "she is going places", they see one example of the motivation that I'm talking about here. In this case that type of motivation is more than likely career driven motivation. Those persons are willing to work more hours, work harder, go the extra mile, pick any metaphorical phrase you want, they are willing to do it. They recognize that doing this "grinding" will make them more competitive or accelerate their progress, and therefore they will do more and better than others who are their peers.

There are many other types of motivation as well that we can also explore. As someone who manages people, or someone who is trying to get a group of others to do something for you, you need to understand people's motivations. I know that sounds simple and may even border on a platitude. However, I want you to have a tool here where are you can academically study someone and attempt to identify their motivation or motivations. If you have a list of motivations to pull from, you can start to understand why one person in a ten-person group will work harder than the others or why these three particular people stay around even though they're working on a tough job.

You'll also recognize when someone is leaving your company or your team, that a lack of motivational alignment is often one of the big drivers for them to leave. And this is probably the most important statement I'll make in this chapter. *In order to assure long term success, you must align people's motivations with your end goal.* No matter how many resources you give someone, how much protection you give them over the period to meet that goal, and how accountable you attempt to make them with your measures, if their personal motivation is not closely aligned with what you're trying to accomplish, they will never be able to truly commit to your program or your effort. They will stay for a short time and eventually leave or perform in a mediocre fashion. It's just human nature.

So, motivation comes in many forms. Sometimes people hold onto a terrible job, only due to motivation. I'll paint a few extreme examples here, so that you understand what I am trying to convey. If someone has 10 children, they have a major problem that they must solve, which is paying for all those children. Kids are wonderful yet expensive. Every time you have another kid, life gets more and more expensive in a significant way. Someone might just have two children and already be financially underwater or at least be in a risky place. So, they get or keep a job, that treats them half decently, or frankly doesn't treat them half decently. It pays the bills, so their personal motivation to pay for those children is enough to keep them with that company. Basically, if they must pay the bills, they're going to hold onto that job as much as they can, because finances are a large part of anyone's personal motivation. In many ways, money controls many people. Until they become financially independent, they still have some part of their personal motivation that is tied to collecting a paycheck or salary. As they build savings and such, and they know that they can replace that salary with less risk, then their personal motivation turns into other things, and finances become less significant in their motivators.

If they are knowledge workers, or they manage knowledge workers, then finances may be less of a concern. The salary at that point is just part of the lowest level of Maslow's hierarchy of needs, where knowledge workers want to be sure they are paid at least at market rate. Once they get paid that, they are looking for other motivators in the organization. There's a wonderful little whiteboard video out there from RSA (Royal Society for encouragement of Arts) that talks all about "Drive: The surprising truth about what motivates us" on YouTube. Knowledge workers are more motivated by challenging work and other benefits that a company can offer. Being in a cool industry is a motivator. When you are hiring someone or when you are searching for a new job, the overall benefits package is important. Interviewing for fit becomes important, because people are looking for a more holistic offer, not just the salary.

One motivator for students coming out of college is often a powerful brand. If you are someone looking for the world's best training programs or a world known brand like a Google, Amazon, or EA, you will work for that company regardless of whether there are things that are not good about it. You'll do it, because you want a stamp on the forehead. You'll do it, because you have always wanted to work in an industry like theme parks, video games, space travel, film, a sport, etc.

What follows is a list of example motivators. Think about these for yourself, and if you are a manager, think about whether any apply to your staff. You can choose which ways you want to proactively motivate your team. However, the study of motivation is deep and wide. I won't replicate that here, as you will be better served by looking into three best-selling books on the topic. The first is *Drive* by Daniel H. Pink, which discusses a common disconnect between what science knows about motivation and what we tend to do in business. The video mentioned above is adapted from David Pink's talk at the RSA. He lays out a wonderful and clear assessment of the three types of motivation (1.0, 2.0, and 3.0). He discusses extrinsic motivators vs. intrinsic motivators. And he discusses the three types of intrinsic motivation: autonomy, mastery, and purpose. If you pick any book to read on motivation, get Pink's book.

The second is *Grit,* by Angela Duckworth, which discusses the mindset of those who take the long-term view of reaching a goal. Loosely related is Simon Sinek's *Start with Why*, which I include, because it talks about how organizations inspire their employees and customers to do great things. But to simply illustrate the point for the purposes of this conversation, here are a few related examples (with Pink's categories in parentheses):

Financial Motivations: (extrinsic)
- College debt
- Pending college purchase for a child
- Purchase of a home
- Huge salaries
- Big bonuses

Medical Motivations: (survival)
- Large family
- Family member with significant medical needs
- Recent surgeries

Career Motivations: (intrinsic)
- Seeking of leadership positions
- On the job training and certifications
- Powerful street cred from a strong brand
- Mentorship

- Challenging work
- Smart teammates
- Control of one's destiny

Social Motivations: (survival)
- Lots of friends at work
- Social engagements like game nights, holiday parties, etc...
- Work/Life balance
- Outreach programs
- Flexible hours

Life & Death Motivations: (survival)
- Soldiers on the frontlines protecting our country must overcome some amazing fears. And so must local heroes like law enforcement and firemen. What do you suppose motivates them?
- A sense of loyalty to the country
- Care for their families
- Protection of their teammates and themselves
- Care for fellow humans

Recognition Motivations: (intrinsic)
- Private thank you from manager and above
- Public thank you in front of team or company
- Being a part of industry publications or patents

- Thought leadership presentations

How to use this information:

Take a moment for each of your teammates and attempt to assess what motivates them. Make a personal note and watch for pluses or minuses that you are correct. You are also welcome to ask them directly, if you are comfortable with doing so. Just be careful not to get into a deep soul-searching conversation that accidentally opens the door to self-assessment. Instead, you can ask "so what do you find most motivating about being here?" This is especially easy to do when you first join an organization and are getting to know everyone.

Then as you learn of significant events in the lives of your staff, consider that their motivations will change. Getting married, graduation, getting a second degree, having children, purchasing a home or car, passing a milestone age like 40, etc. are all examples of life events that can change what your employee needs or values. Consider whether that will make your valued employees want to stay longer with your company, or your team. If you think those changes will open further opportunities that make them consider leaving, examine how you might offer something new that realigns their personal motivations with yours. Often, recruiters reach out to existing employees after they reach a new achievement and court them away with an opportunity that feels more aligned with their new skills and credentials. The employee may simply say, "I wasn't really looking, but they reached out with this cool opportunity that matches my new degree." If you can afford to create a new internal opportunity before the competitors do, then do so. I have personally experienced situations where I did not take proactive action to court my own employees after they completed a new degree, only to have them provide their resignation weeks later and go to a company that was more exciting to them. When I see those resignations come in, I know that no amount of merit-based motivations (raises, bonuses, promotions) will match the excitement of the new company. I've also offered leadership or new research and development opportunities to those recently getting master's degrees when possible to encourage them to stay.

    To visualize how motivation works within the egg & stool metaphor, allow me use a movie scenario from a 1990's classic film that left an impression on me when I was very young. It is extreme, and it will show that, for the most part, no matter what you offer someone, their motivation may be so out of alignment with doing what you're asking, that you'll never foster enough motivation to convince them to do it. On the other hand, one's motivation can be so powerful, they will overcome significant obstacles to accomplish the task. So, let's say I have a large pile of horse dung. My direction for you is to smear it all over your body and walk around in a crowd full of friends and strangers, say in the mall or a concert, for 15-20 minutes bumping into people. Next in the metaphor is resources. Well, you need the fresh, warm dung and something to smear it with; how about your hand? Check. For protection, I promise not to touch or interrupt you. For accountability measures, I will perform a thorough sniff test, because, well, I'm also committed to your success. And for motivation, I'll give you $10.

"Ok let's go!" I say. You look at me incredulously. Oh, I see the motivation isn't right. How about $20? $100? Hmm at some point you might agree to do this for the right monetary motivation. Well take heart, because it so happens, so would Kevin Costner in the classic movie, Robin Hood. Only he didn't need any cash to make it happen. He did it for love. His character, Robin needed to infiltrate Nottingham's castle, surrounded by the Sheriff's police force to see Maid Maryann. He used this clever, smelly gag to offend the police into pushing him away, unwittingly allowing him safe passage past them. He got to pass right into the castle and find his love. His motivations were love and a heroic calling to save Nottingham, which are certainly more powerful than almost any financial motivations I would be willing to offer you for such an act. Now what if I were to ask 70's rock legend, Meatloaf to do the same thing? He'd probably have answered, "I would do anything for love, but I won't do that", proving that not even love motivates everyone.

Stain, Paint, Clear Coat: Respect

When we treat people merely as they are, they will remain as they are. When we treat them as if they were what they should be, they will become what they should be.   -Thomas S. Monson

If you want to be respected by others, the great thing is to respect yourself. Only by that, only by self-respect will you compel others to respect you.   - Fyodor Dostoyevsky

I start this chapter with two quotes, as I discuss two types of respect – one for others and one for self.

When a Carpenter or an Industrial Designer is building a piece of furniture, they generally will do so with a love for their craft. They both will build whatever the furniture is, secure it with the right kinds of devices so that it is sturdy, and then when the time comes to add the polish, they do so with care.

Any furniture designer or craftsman understands the difference between a common piece of furniture and one that is truly remarkable, comes in the subtle details of the craftsmanship of that furniture. That is why I think this portion of the metaphor rings so true to reality. When you are building your cultural stool, this will be a fun piece of work for you.

Figure out how you will protect that stool. Will you use paint? Will you stain it? Will you use a clear coat of lacquer? Whatever you decide is up to you. That will be a creative choice on your part. However, what I encourage you to do is at least apply something to the stool. Don't let the wood stay bare. What this shows is you respect your craft enough to go the extra mile. You respect the piece of work (or culture) you have built enough to protect it. You respect the time you put into building it, and you want to protect it for the long term.

The culture of a team and consequently an organization is built upon one basic thing: respect. Healthy cultures come from a foundation of a healthy respect for self and a healthy respect for others. Poisoned cultures come from an unhealthy respect for self or an unhealthy respect for others.

Here is a real-life example I have experienced myself more than once, unfortunately. A Product Owner, feature owner, or designer is in a meeting with the team. He or she says, "I haven't had the chance to fully flesh out this design, but if you guys could go ahead and get started, here is the general idea. After you've gotten the first round done, we can come back and iterate."

What he or she is actually saying is this: "I have not had or made the time to do my part of this job. I have not considered this portion of my work or this product or this feature to be high priority enough to do my job correctly. However, I don't want to admit I have failed you. I don't want to feel guilty, because you can't move ahead with your portion of the work. So, if I can convince you to get started even just a little bit, I have unblocked you, and I can keep you busy while I go on to do other things. You will essentially do the design work for me while implementing your guess-driven design and then I will come back and tell you what changes to make. This way I can work on other things that I consider important and I can keep you on the hook. So, I get to have my cake and eat it too. I can still accomplish things I care about, and I don't own the guilt of blocking your work."

Teams are often asked to implement products against napkin sketches or shaky designs. The foundation of the decision on the part of the feature owner in this conversation is based on a lack of respect. It can be a combination of both types of lack of respect. He or she does not respect the time the production staff will take to implement that feature. He does not respect the fact people will build something he will reject and want changes on. He does not have enough respect for the team to give them a good design upfront and save them the frustration of churn, which occurs when people change a feature over and over, because they did not get it right the first time or even the second time.

The second lack of respect comes from a lack of respect for self. The feature owner does not respect him or herself enough to tell others, "no". To be honest with himself and say, "I don't have enough time to design the feature properly, so please find someone else." They don't have enough self-respect to tell the boss they lack enough time to get it all done. So, they try their best to keep the pipeline of work unblocked by using the above technique. Someone who really respects themselves and their ability to get stuff done and their ability to deliver quality work on a schedule, will also have enough self-respect to say, "no" or to ask for help. They can say, "I am a very talented and hard-working individual, and I know I can execute on those things asked of me to a certain realistic limit. Beyond that, I am willing to ask for help, and I do not fear being judged. I do not fear being reprimanded for asking for help."

Often, very junior people (whether it is a designer, artist, engineer, manager, etc.) don't know enough about their role or have enough years under their belt in that role to respect themselves enough to say, "no." They don't know enough to confidently determine whether a workload is too much or not.

On the flipside, let's look at the production team or development team being asked to implement the feature. In this meeting, you'll have one of two or three types of individual with varying levels of self-respect. The very senior people who have learned to have a voice in their organization can quickly judge whether what is being asked is realistic. They can see the Product Owner is asking for a freebie. They can see they will do a lot of work, show it to the designer, clearly be wrong in their assumptions, and must rebuild or redesign significant parts of the feature. Those people have enough self-respect to stand up and say, "No, this design is not good enough. I expect more from you as my teammate. Let's iterate on the design first while it is cheap before we build something that is wrong to begin with." They also have enough respect for their teammates to know is an unhealthy approach building any product. They respect their team, especially the junior members, enough to speak up and protect that team.

Some people however regardless of their seniority or juniority, do not have enough self-respect to say anything. They will simply accept this is the way of life, and they will try their best to implement based on their own assumptions and knowledge about the customer. They also will fail, and they may or may not know it. But they have not experienced enough churn, to finally find their voice and defend themselves. If the leadership in the room tolerates this kind of exchange where a leader is allowed to ask for favors from the development team, they are also in the same situation where they do not respect themselves enough to speak up or they do not respect the team enough to protect it. If you have seen meetings go by where no one is fighting to protect the team, and instead everyone just accepts this is the way of life, then you are seeing a situation where self-respect and team respect are low.

In another scenario, I worked with an extremely intelligent and extremely overworked technical lead on a AAA game team. We were in the middle of a heavy "crunch" period trying to prepare the game for shipping. He was a critical path team member, who essentially got most of the extremely difficult problems. Like most of the team, he had working long hours, long days, and long weeks.

There was a point in the cycle where the lead was so frustrated with a teammate's approach to problem solving, he began screaming and insulting the teammate in a hallway full of cubicles. The teammate was not there, but about 20 to 25 other developers were. I asked the lead to come with me to a conference room and explain to me what was going on. He vented all his frustrations there, and I took some actions items to help in the near term. My immediate goal was to get him away from the team, as he had clearly reached a limit of stress and fatigue that he would be willing to scream about someone in front of others. His frustrations were real and needed addressing, but he was also bringing down the morale of his co-workers. I worked with his manager to give him some time off and get refreshed.

    That is not the first time I have seen disrespectful language about others used in a company setting. It normally happens when people are frustrated and tired. Management books call people being "actively disengaged" when they are poisoning culture by complaining openly to others in the company and sewing discontent in general. I have even seen it when people are jokingly talking about a person's mannerisms. They mean it all in good fun, or as a way to vent, but in the end, behavior like this is disrespectful. Doing this in large groups or meetings can cause real morale issues. In those situations, I almost always try to remind myself and them that we are lucky to be working for that team. Sometimes you can remind your team of the good reasons they are working in the company, sometimes it won't matter for some individuals. But in the end, facilitating respect in your organization is definitely a way you can help as a leader.

Healthy cultures are founded on active maintenance of respect. That's easy to say, but as always, actions speak louder than words. By respecting deadlines and feature sets, teams prove they respect themselves and each other enough to protect themselves from buckling under the pressures of time. A healthy team will follow a regular development cycle, with regular quality control, with regular feature cut off dates, and they will ship on time. They will have product designers or feature designers who are realistic about timelines. Those designers, salespeople, business owners, or CEOs, will respect there is only so much time in the day and only so much time in their development calendar to get things done. They will respect the team does not want to grind for the entirety of their tenure in the organization. They will refrain from letting that last-minute temptation to get something amazing in convince them to pressure teams into making bad cultural decisions. And individuals on a team don't complain loudly about things they dislike in the hallways. They take frustrations to their managers and suggest solutions.

Of course, every now and then something out of our control will happen. Something will cause the team to be taken aback and change direction. However, that something should be an aberration. It should *not* be the norm. If randomization and cramming are the norm, your team has an unhealthy culture. You'll have high turnover. Your people will not trust your organization. They certainly won't have respect for it. If, however, you build an organization that puts people first, then forces and encourages them to respect themselves, you'll have a higher level of longevity over the decades.

Force is a strong word, isn't it? In this case, force refers to the protection leg of the stool. You must protect the team from making bad decisions by requiring them to understand you won't get everything done. A healthy culture understands you must make sacrifices to ship a product. Those sacrifices don't always have to be people's personal time. It can simply be a reduced feature set.

Marketing directors, Product Owners, and CEOs, who are desperate to add some little last-minute whiz-bang feature, have not learned the value of long-term planning for the health of their team. Startups will hit a point in their growth from garage to real company where they are struggling to keep up with the opportunity. I respect that… to a degree.

If you're lucky enough to be in a startup where you are struggling to keep up with the market opportunity, then talk with your people. Help them to understand the opportunity you have and reward them appropriately. Respect them. Let them know it won't always be like this. And plan to eventually get to a healthier culture. Otherwise you will burn people out, and they will leave. If you have talent that you really want to keep around, you must ensure they are compensated for the grinding culture they are dealing with until the end of the period of growth. Otherwise they will feel mistreated and simply leave.

Good cultures nurture talent. Good cultures respect their employees. Good leaders proactively say "thank you" as often as they can. Good cultures build relationships for the long term, and they do so starting with respect.

Respect your need for good resources.

If you are a teammate and working against a heavy deadline and you find you don't have the resources to move quickly or completely, you can speak up. Sometimes you may be aware of this, but often times teammates just accept they have the tools they are given and never ask for a better tool. It's harder to make a change in a startup, but you can always try. If you can show you will be faster at your job, maybe you'll get it. In large organizations it's just about being aware enough to ask. Senior people on the team will ask. They know when their tools are poor. It is okay as a teammate for you to raise your hand and talk to your manager or leader and say, "I need a better tool here. Can we afford to get me something better, so I could go faster?" Leaders are all about unblocking their people, or at least they should be. A request for a tool that will make you go faster, is welcome. Respect yourself enough and respect your leadership enough to give your team the opportunity to move more quickly and to give them the opportunity to potentially help you. Leaders like to help, and this is one of the easier ways they can help, if they have the money.

Respect yourself and your team enough to ask for good, consistent direction.

Direction is a taboo subject, if you approach it incorrectly. In a scenario where you are a teammate and you feel the team does not have consistent direction from its leadership, a good way to handle raising your concern is to have a one-on-one with your manager or leaders. Tell them you are confused, feel frustrated (if you do), and feel the team is not consistently going in a single direction. Let them know it feels inefficient, and you feel you could do a better job if the direction for your team was clearer. Try to have a few examples of where things have not gone well in the past and caused you or your team to churn on something or throw away work. With a few examples and approaching your leaders with an olive branch on how you think you could solve the problem, you can have an effective conversation that will help the team for the long run. You could also find being bold enough to raise these concerns will strengthen your personal brand as a leader on the team and as someone who is forward thinking and trustworthy. If you approach the conversation in a humble manner, you're more likely to build bridges rather than burn them down.

    Also stay aware that communications always involve two parties. So, be mindful of the fact you might really just be confused and need to offer that awareness in the meeting. You may find you'll learn something everyone else knows, and therefore direction really *is* clear to the team. But more than likely, if you're confused, someone else is too, and by asking the questions you'll affectively be reminding your leadership to do a better job of communicating directions to the team.

Respect yourself and your team enough to ask for protection.

If upper management, the CEO, the marketing director, the Product Owner, designer, or whoever keeps coming to you "sideways," by making requests of you without talking to your management first, ask them to talk to the manager first. You can initially have a conversation with your leaders or your managers and tell them your plan is to start re-directing those participants to the managers. Most managers will be quite happy to know you are aware enough to see this as a problem and will be more than happy to use themselves as a shield to protect you.

Also, there are kind ways to ask others to do that. You can simply say, "You know that sounds like a great idea, can we put that in front of my manager to ensure it is higher priority than our current workload? If so then I am more than excited to help."

Respect is Silent

Stain and clear coat are one of the most profound parts of this metaphor, and therefore my most favorite. Respect is a silent part of every organization. Or it is not. Its presence, or lack of presence, will pervade the team, whether or not the team is aware enough to look for it. By ensuring you take a moment to gauge whether your team has respect, you will start to change your awareness forever. You will be able to see it. You will be able to see a lack of it. Simply being aware of this element will change how you perceive conversations that go on in the hallway, behind closed doors, and in one-on-ones.

You will know if this is something your team needs real help on. Respect is absolutely one of the strongest contributors to the health of a culture, even if you can't see it yet.

One final note about respect: Consider reading the Credo written by Thomas Gordon in his seminal book on Leadership called Leadership Effectiveness Training (L.E.T.). You can find the credo online at his website. His organization may even send you a copy to frame and place on your office wall. In following that credo, you will find many more people want to stay on your team, simply because they will feel the respect you give them every day.

Fortifiers (Struts)

"There's no doubt that the squad needs strengthening if we are to get back up among the top three, because they are operating on another level to us at the moment." – Steven Gerrard

The initial purpose of the egg and stool metaphor is to give you a framework from which to see all aspect of enabling commitment. If the stool is imbalanced in anyway, the egg falls off and cracks, thus losing commitment to contain all the yolk. Some of the yolk leaks out, and they miss hitting some or all of the stuff they committed to at the beginning of the effort.

A longer-term extension of the egg and stool metaphor is to consider that your employees are the eggs. They are sitting on your stool and by virtue of doing so, they trust your stool and have committed to sitting on it. In this scenario, they have committed to work at your company. After you have built a culture using the egg & stool metaphor of four legs and the seat such that you have provided adequate resources, protection, accountability, support their motivations, and have a unified, consistent direction, what do you do next?

Envision for a moment someone in your organization sitting on your stool. Their bottom is resting on the seat. They are sitting comfortably. Well done. However, their feet are still planted on the ground, which indicates they are not 100% committed to your company yet. Their trust and their ability to sit longer on your stool lies in one more addition to your stool: the struts (or fortifiers). You will know when your teammates fully trust your stool, when they will lift their feet off the ground and rest those feet on the struts you have added to your stool.

This chapter shows you how you can add struts to your stool. These fortifiers make the stool more comfortable to sit on. The more comfortable people are, the longer they will stay. So, how do you make people comfortable?

A bit of artistry naturally emerges from the effort of performing most professions, even technical ones. As humans we all walk different lives, have different mental filters or perspectives on the world, and generally those variables in our thinking can lead to several different outcomes from the same basic task. For example, one engineer may write an amazingly complex piece of code that has no comments and combines multiple operations into single lines. The code may be beautiful to him, quite elegant, extremely efficient, and completely un-maintainable by anyone except him. In the same office, another engineer may value maintainability and code readability over efficiency. Her code may run less efficiently, but it can be read by junior engineers, maintained by other engineers besides her, and may take several lines of operations to do the same things that the other engineer's code did Both engineers may be very pleased with their own creations. For the user, the end functionality is roughly the same. The engineers have used their creativity, personal interests, interest for their team, and/or business needs to create two different pieces of code. It demonstrates the "art" side of an otherwise a mechanically equivalent situation.

You can apply your own sense of art in building your commitment culture too. Yes, you'll have a seat with four legs, but you can add fortifiers to make your culture even stronger, to make your employees trust your organization even more. To give your people reasons to trust your culture. To make it more "stay worthy".

Below are some examples of fortifiers you can add to your commitment culture to strengthen it. It is not an exhaustive list. You will certainly come up with your own. Some of these may seem obvious on a cursory glance; some won't.

Training

One way you can fortify the strength of your culture is by facilitating good training for your teammates, which is different than extended education (discussed later on). There is often an implicit assumption people have competencies in all their required areas. However, many don't.

Imagine an engineer is expected to know how to develop in a certain language. Or perhaps she is expected to know how to develop against a certain architecture. If that engineer is expected to know something she doesn't, she might hide it from the team. She may be too embarrassed to admit she doesn't know something. As a result, she plods along, especially if what she needs to know is not easily learnable. Generally, the reluctance to ask for help (additional training) occurs with younger engineers. They've come out of school, and yes, they have basic training in a variety of technologies and languages and tools, however sometimes academia doesn't quite prepare students for the real world.

By ensuring your engineers have basic training against the tool sets they are supposed to adopt, the technology stack they are supposed to adopt, the languages that they are supposed to be using, and so on, you ensure a level playing field for all of your engineers. If you can lay a foundation where junior engineers are given the resources they need to self-train and are told they are expected to be at a certain level of aptitude, you'll make a huge difference in the skill set and speed of your team.

Aptitude tests help teachers figure out where to place children in school. Your team can benefit from the same technique. When you have a variety of engineers at different levels of skill sets working on your team, you will rarely have the perfect a team. There will be people who don't know a technology stack, who don't know a language, or who don't know a specific tool. One way to figure out what your team knows is when the engineer joins the team or at some point within the year, you have everyone take an exam. You create an exam that addresses basic requirements. The point is not to scare or intimidate people or call out engineers on your team for being inadequately prepared. The point is to ensure your expectations and assumptions about the skill set of your team are accurate. The point is to give you a chance to do something about it.

For example, my background is electrical engineering, so I have learned all my software development skills on the job with the exception of a couple of basic coding classes back in college. Early in my career, I worked for a company that did embedded software development for Microsoft operating systems, I was being asked to do some reasonably savvy development on a Windows CE device. Although I was quite experienced with Assembly, C, and C++ language development, I was not savvy with developing the Windows CE operating system using Visual Studio, the development environment of choice. And worse, I did not know what I was expected to know.

Instead, I had to learn on the fly how to develop in this operating system and how to develop with this development environment. I was too embarrassed to ask for help and as a result, I plodded along. Then one day I was paired with a technical lead. Our manager asked him to show me some basics around getting a problem solved. I took a leap of faith and shared with him that I did not understand how to connect the development environment to the embedded device and get the basic operating system up and running, so I could develop the app we were making. He was stunned. He handled it very well, but he did let his body language communicate he was surprised, and then he kindly proceeded to teach me what I needed to know. Although I was embarrassed in the moment, we got past that. He did however spend more time with me than he had expected in order to ensure I knew what I was doing.

You might think that is a fine way to learn. You might say that is a fine way to teach. You might say that is a fine way to train the people on your organization. You would almost be right.

I have senior people teach junior people all the time. I agree with that one hundred percent. What I don't agree with is allowing people to muddle through because they don't know what they don't know. And, more importantly, you don't either.

A smarter plan is to perform these assessments during a given year especially when someone has just joined your team. Let them know you're not going to punish them, if you find they don't know something. Instead, you'll build a plan or provide them with resources they can use to teach themselves. Put time in your schedule for them to learn this stuff. It seems obvious, but I have seen time and time again where engineers and artists are not given ample time to train on a new technology.

Here's another example from much later in my career. At this point, I was a fairly senior project and career manager for engineers, technical artists, and junior managers. I recently joined a team, where a very junior engineer was struggling. He had been hired fresh out of college, and according to two senior technical leads, during the interview he showed much promise. Six months after being hired, it was clear he was underperforming. A lot of it had to do with soft skills, but he also did not have much skill with C++. He could not debug memory issues, call stack issues, nor really use the development environment very well. He had become a drain on the technical lead, who was shouldered with the responsibility of guiding his work.

At the six-month point, the technical lead was tired of trying. *The junior engineer did not even know he was doing a bad job.* They were not communicating well. Because he was hired as a contractor, he was almost let go from the company. This was happening just as I took over the team. I stepped in, and helped find the issues, recognizing there were issues on both sides. We were able to set this junior engineer back on a path of success.

However, if the team had already been set up to assess this new engineer's skill set, they would have quickly recognized the gaps in his knowledge. They would have provided time for him to train. And in doing so he would have been less of a drain on the technical lead. Or, in another scenario, more training should have been provided to the people who hired him about how to identify more qualified talent.

These days when training career managers and leads responsible for interviewing, I teach them to assess each candidate for what they bring to the job with them and what the company will need to invest in them. When your interviewers approach assessing a candidate that way, it is a more even assessment and creates a better environment for getting to know a candidate.

One way to do assessment and training is simple. As a technical lead, engineering manager, or project manager, you build a few basic projects. Those projects are training programs designed to teach the engineer how to do basic memory leak checks, missed handles, basic architecture, and to use the tool in a variety of basic ways such as call stack debugging and so on. There are also courses out there you can pay for right off the shelf that will do this for you. You also need a checklist. You put the checklist in front of the engineer, and you tell the engineer, "You are expected to know how to do these 10 things to be effective on this project. Please take this test and tell me what you were not yet prepared to do. Then, we'll lay out a plan to get you performing at this level."

Is this a lot of work? Yes.

Cultural investment by leadership often just takes manpower. It takes time away from your day-to-day grind to invest in the future of your organization. So, you do it in bits and pieces. Often, you can get the team to help.

Here's an example for managers. I often get the impression managers are expected to have all the answers. That they have somehow reached a point in their careers where they are no longer expected to make mistakes, and they no longer need training. Years ago, during interviews, I started asking the question, "What can I learn if I work for you?" Often times those performing the interview don't have an answer. If their mindset seems to be, "Well you are an executive leader, and if you need to learn something, I can't trust you with my team", that's a red flag.

Among the courses I have taken, two significantly changed the way I manage my teams and the way I encourage my managers to run theirs. And considering how many people a career manager can affect, training your managers is extremely important. The first training is with a program called LeaderPoint. In one sentence, LeaderPoint taught me about the value of delegating tasks and work to my team. In more detail, it taught me how to set my teams expectations that they could be leaders too, and that they could self-organize. Before this training I thought that my value as a manager was my ability to take on as much overhead work as possible, so my developers didn't have to do it. I also thought I had to make all the big decisions for the team. I had not yet understood the poor service I was causing to the team by getting caught in the day-to-day grind and not be able to rise above my team to assess the large cultural problems. This training helped me to understand the power of delegation and the power of setting my team up to be able to run without my involvement in the day-to-day activities. I was learning to lead instead of manage. Over the years I regularly meet managers who cannot yet delegate. They carry mountains, and their team cannot run without them. This step from managing to leading is a natural step in most career paths. *If you set your culture up correctly, your team will not need you to be there in order to succeed.*

Ramp-Up Procedures

One of the best ways to ensure new hires on your team feel comfortable with their decision to join you or your company is to give them the best chance to succeed during the first few weeks they arrive. People usually take about a month to assess their decision to join a new company. Therefore, it is critical to quickly strengthen their integration into your team, to the point they will feel well taken care of. This is one of my favorite struts to add to any organizations cultural stool, because it's also one of the cheapest to do.

Many teams fail to create a ramp up experience that ensures everyone's knowledge is equivalent to everyone else's with respect to the context of the job, tool sets, common procedures, people to ask questions, and cultural concerns. Generally, there are a couple of hours of orientation performed by human resources on day one and then the person is handed off to their manager. That manager normally assigns a technical lead as a "buddy" to help get the new person's tools set up and answer questions in the first week or so of employment. That's a good start. It can cover the basics of what a new employee needs to get integrated from a resources standpoint.

Welcome Document

A welcome document that has been built by the team to share knowledge with the new hire is an excellent next step. This welcome document describes nuances with backend systems (such as timecards), documentation websites (like confluence), project management tools, domain knowledge they should have, and even things as basic as where to find office supplies. Yes, that's possibly silly to some people. You might just assume they will figure that stuff out by themselves, or someone will tell them and yes eventually, someone will tell them. But it is much nicer to prepare for the common questions, by creating a simple document that says, "Welcome to our team, here are all the basics you will need to know in joining us."

Sometimes these welcome documents are called tribal knowledge documents because they should be built by the community on your team. In fact, the very first task you give the new person should be to fill in missing information they wish had been in the document when *they* joined. It's a great way for them to feel taken care of and to immediately contribute to the team by helping the next person who is going to come on the same journey.

If you are a leader looking for another tip, make your own checklist of things to do for this new hire during their first week. Share it with leaders you are training, to help them do a better job with ramp up. I use mine to catch the little things that normally are delayed or are found out by the new hire as they try to get resources like access to shared servers. Getting ahead of these things will show your new hire they are important from day one.

Training Videos

You often see training videos from HR in an organization. These are intended to train someone on the legal concerns that the company has around harassment, appropriate workplace behavior, cyber-security, and so on, but they can also be leveraged to improve your new hires' ramp-up. Documentation (like confluence pages) are worth the number of words on the page (or less). Pictures are worth 1000 words. Videos are worth 1 million.

Don't believe me? Think about how much you can learn to do on YouTube, from home repair to coding. Your new hires will appreciate having engaging videos to help them learn how to do simple things, like log in to your bug tracking system and get a bug or track their hours in the project management system against a story. Videos can also teach them what the cultural expectations are around your project management methodology are good too. As an example imagine a video where your new hire learns what the development cycle looks like for your team, what your core hours are, so people know when to expect others in the office, and what methods of communications are common with the team such as email, meetings, slack, documentation websites, and so on.

The most important thing about videos is that they multiply your effort. If you invest the time to create a training video once, you don't have to retell the same thing 10 times when 10 new hires join. They can watch the video as needed, and you can move on to do other things with your culture. One might say the same for documentation, which is true, except videos are much more engaging than documentation.

Managers who prefer to go over these during on-on-one meetings can follow a checklist to reduce human error.

Make it Official

I like to put a week or two "ramp up" task right in the project schedule for someone, so it is clear to them and everyone else where they are and what the expectations are. I often tell my engineers to not expect to code anything for one week. Just to be patient.

I also recommend scheduling a one-on-one with your new hire a week after they join if not sooner, depending on your situation. Plan to give them the opportunity to fill in gaps. Plan to get feedback from them, so you can make the next new hire's experience even better. Take care of your new hires, as winning their confidence now helps them to more easily "sit on the stool" for the long term.

Commit to This Yourself

Even in an environment, like consulting, where people need to jump from one project to another, there are still ramp up tasks that need to happen as someone is learning about your new project. If your gut reaction is, "Yeah that sounds great, but I just don't have time right now to improve ramp-up procedures", that is an indicator you are too deep in the weeds to be running your team. If you spend 10 or 15 minutes each week putting pennies in your ramp-up piggy bank, you will eventually have thousands of dollars' worth of training value. You can give this value to new hires to make sure they feel well treated by the organization when they join AND have their knowledge on-level with the team.

Extended Education & Personal Growth

Often, people are expected to go learn something new on the job. Engineers are technically savvy people. As an example, they must often learn a new language, if they're developing software or firmware. Or they may need to learn a piece of hardware, new tools, etc. If the organization has the resources, i.e. money available, it is often worth the expense to pay for that person to get some extended education. Managers can get management training. Engineers can get engineering training. Artists can get tool and creative training. Training may be on tools or methodologies. Although this is probably obvious, and you're wondering why I am referring to it, I rarely see employees take the opportunity. Even more rarely, do I see managers *encouraging* their employees to grow by doing something relevant and asking for training dollars. If anything, they broadcast a message about benefits that HR provides, but never ask individuals to bring a training opportunity specifically to the manager for review. By asking, you will show you care enough to fortify your organization with personal growth.

Communications

Hands down, one of the most common problems teams must repeatedly solve is communications. In the early days of an organization, it is just about establishing norms. Later, as teams grow, it is about handling the multiple directions communications can take and ensuring people don't get confusing or untimely information.

Surveys have shown one of the skills managers prize the most when hiring individual contributors, is the ability to communicate well. Below are ways to fortify your stool with better communications.

Shared Vocabulary

If you have reasonably mature communication skills, it is relatively easy to translate technical jargon into common jargon. I was once asked in a Microsoft interview how I would explain to my grandmother what I did in a telecommunications engineering position as a co-op. That question has always stuck with me as a quintessential test of one's communications soft skills.

Laypeople normally do not care about the nitty-gritty details of what you're trying to accomplish, unless they are trying to accomplish similar goals and have comparable levels of savvy in whatever technical effort you are trying to drive. That's true for any engineering, or other technical effort. For example, my eyes will glaze over if my wife, a doctor, goes into too much technical detail about how psychological issues may play out in the life of someone who has a very complicated situation. In that context, she's the expert, and I'm the layman.

However, this ability to translate jargon into layman's terms is a communication skill that must be learned. When you're steeped in a technical field at all times, it's difficult to remember not everyone knows the jargon.

This often comes up when engineers are trying to give me a status update that I must then convert into a summary status for people further removed in management. In this scenario, the higher up managers do not care about all of the details. They need to understand the schedule impacts of the engineers' challenges on the business. So, my job on a recurring basis is to convert technical detail into business level statements for upper management. This is commonly referred to as the executive summary. The higher up in the management chain you go in an organization, the smaller the amount of information needs to be. Brevity is required to be useful. And it's not because the people higher up in the managerial change are less intelligent or less trained than someone on the lower rungs of the organizational hierarchy. In fact, most CFOs have financial degrees and MBAs, and they are wielding an entire organization affecting millions of dollars, if not billions. *The purpose of brevity is to save those people time.*

Generally speaking, any minute of wasted time at that level can lead to hundreds or thousands of dollars of wasted money. They don't need the details. They don't want the details, because they can't spend the time.

If you come back to the level where an engineer is speaking with a person in a different technical domain, for example an artist, while making some user interface or game, they need to find a common ground. An engineer who is technically savvy at his work speaking to an artist who is technically savvy at her work, need to share common vocabulary. That common vocabulary supports good communications. This is often done with a WIKI or other document that captures the industry or company jargon.

Mechanisms

In addition to common vocabulary, communications mechanisms are also important. Email is the most common solution, but it is not necessarily the best solution to good communications. In fact, if I could eliminate email altogether from my world and my teams' worlds, I would do it in a heartbeat. We would be more effective.

Many people feel the same way about meetings. Managers are in meetings all the time, and engineers and other individual contributors hate meetings, because they seem so inefficient. The truth is they *are* often inefficient and wasteful. Email is also inefficient and wasteful. So, we also have other communications mechanisms like Confluence and Wiki, project management tools, Skype and other chat tools (like Slack), that attempt to eliminate email and some of the challenges with it.

All of these mechanisms have fans. Any given individual will prefer one mechanism over the other. That is because communications, like many other things that we do, is an art form.

Common Problems

The problem with art forms is that beauty is in the eye of the beholder. Whereas I cannot stand to use email, there are people on my team who absolutely love it and believe they can get everything accomplished in an email. However, if they do not write the email very well, inefficiencies begin, and their goals do not get accomplished. This happens very often on large teams, where people have not been taught how to communicate over email. Email can be easily lost, get multithreaded or "splintered", get jumbled, and become so long no one wants to read it. There is even a common acronym, "TL;DR," that describes the emails no one reads. It stands for "Too Long; Didn't Read."

Problems like poorly written emails, poorly arranged meetings, poorly written technical documents, and development stories, docs, etc. can be helped. Communications training is simple. However, many leaders and or teammates overlook it. They believe they already know how to communicate, because they can get by. However, getting by with the basics, or "muddling through" is where the problem starts.

Bad communications are emails that are not directed to anyone. They have a large group of people on the To and CC lists and yet when that person starts this body of the email, the body says "Hey," and rambles on for two or three paragraphs. This is the equivalent of someone standing on a street corner and rattling off his or her needs to a group of passersby. No one will listen or reply.

Bad communications are when you leave a meeting, and no one has taken any notes. When people nod their head in agreement, they have an action item and yet they don't write it down, that's a solid sign they will not take the action after all. When people are quite content to leave a meeting without following up on their action items, that is bad communications. As a leader, you should hold people accountable for those bad communications and their lack of commitment. Regularly encourage and expect everyone to bring a pad and pencil to the meeting.

When people are checking code into a software database for source control management, and they are not adding comments as to why they're checking this code in, that's bad communication. They're not holding themselves accountable to documenting why they are doing whatever it is they are doing. When people are working on things and there is nothing to track what they are working on, such as a task in a task management system, that's bad communication.

Body language is one of the most commonly overlooked methods of communication. As a manager, studying body language is an excellent practice, because it can tell you a lot about your teammates. For example, you can tell when someone is not happy with what is going on or that they have simply "checked out" of what the conversation is about. They do not believe the conversation applies to them or aligns with their views, and therefore they don't engage. Then when time for accountability rolls around, they act like it was never part of their responsibility in the first place.

As a manager, it can be difficult to help your team improve their body language, but sometimes there are cases when you can step in. Study body language first, so you can identify risk. Then later as you get at reading, understanding, and proactively using body language, you can confidently mentor others.

Addressing Communication Problems

Communication is absolutely one of the most critical skills anyone can learn. Your team needs to be able to communicate well. And if they cannot, it is up to you as a leader to fix that problem. If you add a clear expectation that one's ability to communicate is considered a premium on your team, then you will get better communications. Here are some things you can do to strengthen your team's ability to communicate.

First, ensure they understand they are expected to do it very well. Give them examples of bad communications and good communications. For example, with emails, start with your own emails ensure that every single time you write an email, someone's name is called out when you were asking something, or when you are telling them to do something. Every. Single. Time.

You can use brick red to call out individuals' names. Brick red is good because it helps people to quickly scan the email for their name to see if it is specifically calling on them. And then they can respond. Avoid bright red, because it is a very aggressive color. Email is so easy to misconstrue meaning, you don't want to be aggressive with it.

Encourage your teammates to always call out someone's name when they send mass emails. Don't let your people send headless emails. Kindly reply to them directly when they do so and encourage them to put someone's name in that email. Doing so provides on the job training for good communications via email.

As far as communicating they are required to own their own action items, make sure everyone on your team has easy access to a notebook and pencil from day one. When you walk someone around the office ramping them up, take them to the office supply cabinet and give them a notebook and a pencil. You can say, "Please bring this notebook and pencil to every meeting." In meetings you look around and say politely, "I don't see that everyone has a way to take notes. Do you guys need some supplies?" You can remind people individually in one-on-ones.

It is important for you to tell people that you are serious when it comes to good communications. By giving them resources they need, holding them accountable for good communications, and following up to help when they neglect it, you're setting up the culture for success. There's no real reason to be lazy in a meeting. You can also follow up with your own email meeting notes and call out people individually for action items in the same way as you call out their names with questions and emails per my description above. But encouraging people to take notes during meetings is basic.

As for body language, I've had more than one instance where I helped an engineer improve his or her body language for the benefit of the team. In one instance I had a very physically large individual, who was intimidating a much smaller individual, not only with his body language, but also with his verbal communications, facial affect, and tone of voice. He was a very technically savvy person and so was the smaller individual. But the smaller individual was just quieter & smaller and therefore intimidated by all the variables in that communication scenario. As a result, the more dominant person won the conversation and got his way for a design. But he caused the less confident engineer to be less vocal the next time around. Had it continued, the smaller engineer would have felt increasingly alienated from the team and therefore might have left.

I had meetings with both of engineers about body language. We discussed body language and nonverbal communications and respect for each other and self. Those are very soft skill driven conversations. However, soft skills can make all the difference in someone's career trajectory. The aggressive engineer was never going to get to the next level of his career, by being someone who intimidated others. The junior engineer was never going to get to the next level of his career, if he backed down every time he was called out on an idea. They had to find a middle ground, so they could both move forward as a team to be successful.

As a leader, teach yourself about body language and then teach your teammates about body language. If you manage managers, discuss this skillset regularly and suggest books on the subject. Body language is just another powerful form of communication, and if you make it a priority in your teachings to your team, you can really empower your team for success.

Secondaries (or Backups)

Imagine a scenario where there is an individual on your team that you dread losing. This individual is so critical to your organization's success, that if anything happens to them, your company will suffer delays to the tune of weeks or months. If this person were to be hit by a bus and not come in tomorrow, your group would be in real trouble (some people describe this as a "high bus factor"). You might be able to get by or limp along, but they contain critical knowledge no one else does. There is no one on the team who can possibly do their job as efficiently or adequately as they can. Obviously, this is a risky scenario to find yourself in for a couple of reasons.

First, these people are generally highly paid, and their level of job security is also very high. Unfortunately, that may encourage them to behave like a prima donna and believe everything they say should be adhered to or followed.

The bigger risk is that this person is mission critical. They cannot take a day off. They cannot get away from work without significantly impacting the team. Therefore, they are often stuck working more hours than most people, especially when times get hard, and they cannot get anyone to give them relief. If they are the only one who can solve a given problem, work on a specific technology, or within a specific system, it puts the individual at high risk of exhaustion and the team at a higher risk for failure.

The solution is investment. Investment is simple: perform cross training. Cross training, even to a small degree, will help alleviate this critical path situation for individuals and managers. In this scenario, appoint another member on their team as their "secondary" or "backup" for an area of knowledge. Ensure they continually discuss the ins and outs of that area, whether it's code, an entire feature set, a kind of technology, a managed team, or whatever. You can ensure they are communicating by requiring the secondary to do reviews on the primary's work. You can divvy up tasks between them as well. One person can still be the primary contributor. That is fine, and it is efficient.

To have another engineer know a reasonable amount about the first engineer's domain can seem redundant, especially if the amount of work necessary to do the job is only one engineer's worth of work. But by ensuring both engineers understand the domain, you ensure neither of them is mission critical. It is worth the investment to reduce the primary person's bus factor.

You may face roadblocks to cross training, such as a program manager who doesn't want to spend dollars training up someone new when someone else already has the knowledge. However, this cross-training is critical protection for the company.

Though large teams are at risk for high bus factor individuals, it is a problem more commonly faced by small teams. The team members each have different areas to cover, and often don't have time to overlap and cross train. On small teams like this, have everyone cross-train and document regularly to help ensure knowledge is transferred.

For leaders and managers, you can ensure knowledge overlap by having them attend the same meetings, always be copied on the same emails, and always joined in the same chat channel. That way, when the main manager must take a day off, the secondary manager can come in and keep things moving forward. Again, it may seem redundant to have two managers in the same meeting, but doing this keeps both managers from being mission critical and allows the team to get to know both managers in the process. However, this does NOT mean there should be "managerial overlap," where multiple managers are asking teammates for the same data. That *is* wasteful of everyone's time. You can have a main manager who does the day-to-day work for their domain and lets the secondary just be a fly on the wall.

The next time you have someone who has a high bus factor, get them a secondary, and put small processes in place to protect the person from being mission critical. They will have a better life balance for it, and your team will be better protected in case the primary must take time off or leave your organization.

Team Building Exercises

Team building exercises are probably the most common and obvious fortifier you can add to your cultural stool. These events help build rapport among people who rarely see each other on a day to day basis. Large organizations often neglect these to their detriment. Plus, team building doesn't have to mean scaling rope ladders and doing trust falls. A friend of mine who owns a small business, regularly takes the entire company (which is about 20 people at this point) out to have dinner and to paint canvases in a local art class. I see the paintings regularly posted on Facebook, which proves it's fun and compelling enough to share afterwards. His company has a culture with one of the strongest retention rates I have seen.
You can search for team building exercises online. Some are available for free as a set of instructions. Others are services you can purchase where you have someone come on site or where you take your team to an offsite event.

A work-sponsored community outreach program is a wonderful cultural program that allows individuals to contribute to the outside community. There are lots of community facilities that would enjoy a hand from an outreach program at your organization, like the Boys and Girls Club or Habitat for Humanity. You can encourage employees to participate by paying them as if they were at work. It's an easy win-win for them and for your company. Your company wins because it is providing a service to the community, and you can use that as news for your company's newsletter. The other win is that you are providing a way for your employees to give back to the community. In exchange for that investment away from official work, they get the psychological income one gets when one helps others. There is something very powerful about helping others. It makes us feel good about ourselves and makes us feel good about the community. It teaches us something, and it builds our bond not only with the community outside the organization but the community inside the organization to.

One of the simplest (and effective) team building activities is having meals together. Research shows people bond when they eat together. We are social animals. Eating together is a social event. Doing so somehow tears down some basic walls between us as animals and builds bonds of trust. Alice Julier examines this in her book, *Eating Together*. Organizing a meal is also one of the easiest things you can do as a leader. Organize a monthly luncheon or have a weekly lunch and learn. Lunch and learns are a wonderful way to help the community in your organization share knowledge.

At one company, our lunch and learns were around process. We did a brown bag scenario, where people volunteered time and presentations. That was okay, but it only led to the hard-core individuals wanting to produce content and come to lunch.

At another organization, we had a chapter of Toastmasters (a public speaking organization). The company paid for the Toastmasters fees and provided lunch. This was very compelling, because it kept people coming to the meetings and staying connected. They could come and watch others who wanted to present and hopefully join the organization and present as well.

Free lunch is a small way to give employees the nod from your organizational leadership that you support their team.

Sometimes you can treat an entire event. For example, in one organization, we went with a team of about forty people to a swanky bowling alley that had drinks, buffets and three dedicated lines to meet our bowling needs. It was fun, and it created a good story later. I met people from our team in Canada. For many of the team, we did not know each other beforehand, but we felt a bond afterwards. We spoke about family and personal ambitions. We learned who could bowl and who could not. It was fun and lighthearted. Faces became stronger than names. Most importantly, it wasn't something awkward, obvious, or trite.

The risk you take in throwing a team building exercise is that it can come off as obvious or trite. In doing so you might undermine the goal of the event in the first place, so be cautious about picking your team building events. If you get the sense from your intuition a team building event is obvious on the surface, or will feel awkward, it probably will. Trust your gut.

A way to generate ideas is to ask around. See if your employees have something they would like to do. Here are some ideas:
- Theme park day
- Trip to see a summer blockbuster
- Dinner cruise
- Social hour at the office (with drinks and music)

Building your team culture using this fortifier can be fun. It can also be expensive, but you can be careful and frugal and do small things. The big things can be more expensive and less frequent. The outreach things can be a great way to connect your employees to your company. And of course, strike a balance between the frequency of these events and their interference with work. Like all of the fortifiers, you can pick and choose which fortifiers you focus on. If you are a big fan of outreach or team building, and you believe that it is one of the best ways to keep your employees happy at work, then this fortifier is for your stool.

I've only given you a few examples here, because books already exist around teambuilding. I encourage you to go online and learn more about what you can do to connect your employees psychologically with their friends at work and with your company.

Décor

In working in large and small companies, open working spaces, cubicle farms, startups and conglomerates, commercial and government companies, I have seen a variety of building décor. I learned along the way that décor really matters in building commitment to your company. I have seen only a handful of organizations that truly understand this, and two of them were entertainment companies. Walking into work every day and seeing eye-popping décor can make employees feel as though they are a part of something truly grand and unusual. This feeling will be something that they must give up when going to a different company. The largest company I worked for to date is EA SPORTS. Their décor in the Vancouver location and the Orlando location is on par with any Disney or Universal Studios, although it is sports themed. Entire walls of nothing but helmets, jerseys, and sports quotes and paraphernalia reinforce how great their products are and how lucky you are to be working on those legendary games. Their Vancouver office had a Feng Shui expert design that location such that employees feel like they are walking around a riverbank and are encouraged to take a stairwell surrounded in glass looking out over the forest surrounding the building. Your company doesn't have to be a Fortune 500 company to do this though. The first company I worked for out of school was a lifestyle business with a sole founder. His sense of design in that first location made you feel like you were working in a home office, complete with beautiful wallpapers, chair rail, paintings, posters, etc. Recently the company outgrew that location and moved to a new building. He invested heavily in a TIKI bar complete with a fully choreographed light show, sound show, storytelling, etc. where voodoo masks tell you all about the drinks you can get at the bar. One of his uses is to entertain themed entertainment customers who visit, but the company employees also get to use it for company parties. There rest of the building has cute wall placards with comedic messages, a workout room, a game room, etc. It really is a sight to behold, and one that inherently makes you smile walking in the door.

  On the other hand, I have seen many organizations that have cubicle farms with white walls only covered with an old marketing poster here and there. This certainly meets the basics of the business, but it does not offer a compelling reason to stay. Invest your time to make the employees' home away from home somewhere they really want to stay. For modern ideas, look at décor from co-working spaces to get you started. Those often have cheap, but refreshing décor, bright colors, etc.

Hiring Process

Another fortifier that strengthens your culture is a good hiring process. The key to a good hiring process is to invest a decent amount of time in identifying and documenting who you want on your team and the role they will fill.

If you have ever been a part of a hiring frenzy, such as what occurs when you are ramping up a team for a large project, then you probably have seen or helped some bad hires join your organization. Bad hires categorically come in two areas.

Lacking Technical Skills

Most companies will give a new hire a de facto grace period to overcome the learning curve associated with a new job. Sometimes the learning curve is technical skills, sometimes it is overcoming the specific learning curve of how a product is made, and sometimes it's simply overcoming tons of terminology that are special to the company or industry. Whatever the case, the company should be aware of the kind of learning curve this person will be on, so that they can correctly judge when the person should be up to speed and "holding their own." This is when they will be performant enough to justify their paycheck by adding the correct amount of value to the product or service.

The first type of bad hire is one who does not have the technical skills for the role, even though they performed well in the interview and seemed to pass the technical challenges. In this scenario, several months into that person's tenure on the team, their lack of skills or training starts to show. Their skills do not match the requirements. As a result, the lead who is put in charge of their ramp up ends up carrying that person more than they should. The new hire becomes a drain on the team. Eventually the lead will ask the manager for help. They may complain they cannot get their job done, because the new hire is weighing them down. That is a cry for help. It also only takes a lead or reasonably senior person on the team going through this once or twice to be able to recognize it more quickly in the future. Whatever the case they eventually will come to you as a manager and ask for help. You then either must decide to invest in this new hire or make a tough decision and let them go. That's a judgment call.

The one thing you should take away from the situation is an action item to find out why they got through the interview process and were invited to join your team. That is your homework. Someone on the technical interview side failed to filter this person. The impact of this mistake is two-fold. The first is that your team's momentum is slowed down. That's the obvious one, and it is the one most leaders and managers are concerned with. The second is that you have also set this person up for failure. If you choose to let them go, you are essentially saying they failed to perform at your requirements. That may be true, but if you and your team had done a great job of interviewing for the right candidate, this person would never have been put in a position to fail. By interviewing poorly, you or your technical lead have set this person up for failure. If you believe in always putting people first, it is your responsibility to ensure the people who join your team are technically capable of doing the job. Otherwise you have hurt your team, and you have hurt that individual.

Poor Cultural Fit

The second categorical mistake that frequently occurs in interviews is one of soft skills and cultural fit. The reason this happens so often, is probably because people really do not understand how to interview for cultural fit. Let's compare two famous (or perhaps infamous) company cultures.

Amazon intentionally breeds an atmosphere of competition, where business units are only encouraged to work together to solve needs if one business unit can convince the other they are worthy of the second business unit's time. Contrast that with EA, where central teams are eager to share the tech and services they provide to game teams in an effort to make better games.

Those are strikingly different cultural approaches. Which is better? Since each culture has pros and cons, it's not for me to generalize. I simply want to highlight they are different, and it is your job to know it. As someone who is performing an interview, you must understand your company's and team's corporate culture. If you do not, you are doing your company (and the individuals you hire) a disservice.

I experienced the tail end of a bad hire a few months into one of the projects I was on. I didn't hire this person, but instead, I inherited him onto my team. I quickly discovered no one had done a culture interview with him. He was only interviewed by technical staff, which unfortunately did not include the technical lead assigned to ramp him up. Within two weeks, it was clear the new hire had social issues, maybe even psychological issues, that were clearly destroying his relationship with the technical lead who was assigned to ramp him up. This technical lead was one of the nicest people I have ever worked with. He was extremely professional, very low-key and tremendously approachable. For him to come to the management office and say he could not train the new hire, was quite a statement. The company culture was technically very savvy, and passionate about the product, but it was not aggressive. In contrast, this person was a very aggressive person. His body language, facial affect, and direct verbal interactions were so bizarre compared to anyone I have ever worked with, it was clear almost from the beginning we were in trouble. I negotiated with his manager and his technical leads to give him three weeks to iron things out. I gave him clear and direct feedback, so he knew the things he needed to improve upon. I worked with him and tried to coach him to get him past these cultural misfits. At the end of three weeks the team was no better, his relationship with his technical lead was no better, and he was not performing well in any sense of the word. I had the unenviable situation of letting him go. That was a terrible experience. I saw the team suffer, and I thought ahead for this person. He was now going to have to explain to his future employers why he only stayed a couple of months at the company. We had handed him a failure. We had wasted money for our team by hiring him. It was an obvious cultural fit failure. We did this because no manager was in the room interviewing the candidate.

Look around your team. Do you see people who stand out as always struggling to fit in? Who seem to do okay at their job, but they are not superstars? If you're not sure why, watch them for a little bit. See if it has to do with their technical skill set or whether they just don't fit in.

Cultural fits are where we get our psychological income. Yes, at a job you do make monetary income. However, psychological income is a huge part of why people join companies and definitely why people stay at or leave companies. Often if someone is going to leave a company, it is due to a frustration somewhere or feeling they just don't belong. When the culture does not support the psychological income needs of the individual, you have a cultural misfit. They will eventually leave.

When you're interviewing, do some homework on your corporate culture. Check out "Who" by ghSmart, a consulting company. They have a plan you can use to in a methodical manner to find "A level" candidates. Part of their interview process includes cultural fit analysis. This is a fortifier for your culture. Can you strengthen your culture by finding the right people to solve the right problems while fitting into the culture? If so, then this fortifier should be a conscious part of the stool you are building.

Other Fortifiers

Of course, there are many other fortifiers you can also consider, such as providing employees with support during hard times, career management services, or how your company handles PTO (Paid Time Off) or vacation.

Companies that go the extra mile supporting a teammate during a hard time (like after surgery or a death in the family) often find it's an amazing way to build loyalty.

Employees who know there is a career trajectory within their organization are also more likely to feel comfortable sitting on your stool. An approach to career management that is solid, academic, and conscientious helps.

There are also novel approaches to vacation time, like a "No PTO" policy. Companies, like Virgin, let you take what you want. Employees are unlikely to abuse fortifiers like this because it makes them feel respected by the company, and generates respect for the organization in turn

Do your research. Create fortifiers you think will help strengthen your commitment culture. These are also things you can highlight during interviews to set your company's culture apart. You can create a cutsheet or marketing slick to give to interviewees during hiring that lists why it is great to work for your company.

A Side Note: False Fortifiers

You can't fake quality any more than you can fake a good meal.
- William S. Burroughs

Imagine you tried to build one of your stool struts out of cardboard. It might look okay at first glance, but it would break as soon as you put any weight on it. False fortifiers are like that. Usually management's heart is in the right place, but these initiatives can easily backfire. An example is "swag" or "street cred."

Giving out swag (t-shirts, posters, certificates, plaques, etc.) for reaching milestones is good. It's exciting to give these gifts, and it is also exciting to receive them. However, if you only give street cred to some members of your team and not others, you create a divide in your culture. For example, say a company only gives swag to their full-time employees and refrains from giving it to contractors. The company justifies the decision by saying it needs a way to reward full time employees who don't get paid for overtime, like contractors do. They do this even though it is clear that most of the contractors really just want to be full-time and are hoping to prove themselves "worthy" enough to land a coveted full-time position.

Treating full-timers as special and contractors as second-class citizens creates a culture where the contractors who work just as hard as the full timers are alienated. Imagine you are on a team that celebrates a milestone by giving full-timers T-shirts. The T-shirts allow full-timers to proudly show they are on your team by walking through the hallways wearing their T-shirt. Now imagine a contractor who is also on that team but is not given a t-shirt. That contractor is likely to feel alienated each time they see someone wearing one of those T-shirts. It's a daily reminder the contractors are not *really* a part of the team.

This is a false fortifier, because it seems like a great idea to reward your team with a cheap but powerful badge of belonging. However, you are alienating the other half of your team. A stool built with this fortifier will cause your contractors to always trust your organization less. They will always keep their feet on the floor, waiting for the stool to break.

Commitment: The "Dramper" Formula

For the things of this world cannot be made known without a knowledge of mathematics. - Roger Bacon

Imagine you are hiring a candidate, and you ask them to commit to working for your organization for 40 years. It is a very rare individual (one that you may not really want) who will sign up for this level of commitment without knowing you. Instead, most hires are made with the implicit assumption you're asking people to commit for the near term (a year or two). Then as you regularly prove your organization will take care of the person's needs, they will continue to stay on an ongoing basis, which could eventually lead to a twenty-year (or more) tenure with you. Essentially, short-term commitments turn into mid-term commitments, which turn into long-term commitment.

Let's focus on the more tangible, short-term periods, so you can see how commitment works on a week-to-week basis. I have built a simple mathematical formula that shows how the major portions of the stool paradigm apply to an individual's commitment to your goal.

My major requirement is to have commitment range from zero to 100%. For those of you who fall asleep at the mention of math, stick with me. You already know what the major pieces are in the metaphor. The purpose here is to cement in your mind an easy way to recall *how* each of the major pieces affect commitment.

So, here's the shorthand (sounds like "see equals dramper"):

```
C = D(R+A+M+P+r)/5
```

Here's the wordy version:

```
Commitment =
Direction*(Resources+Accountability+
Motivation+Protection+respect)/5
```

Here's what it means:

A person's level of commitment to a project (or team) is directly affected by the amount of consistent direction, resources, accountability, motivation, protection, and respect they are given. Dividing these five items by five simply performs an average of their impact, giving them each a chance at contributing something to commitment. Note that direction is the only element that can completely eliminate commitment. When set to zero, meaning there is no direction whatsoever, commitment to deliver on the goal set forth in that direction can only be zero. Any one of the remaining items, when not present, can only reduce commitment by a limited amount.

Here are some concrete ranges for what each of those items means:

D = 0 to 100%: 0 means direction has never been given or is changing by the hour. 100% means direction was crystal clear and did not change throughout the entire period. Leadership stayed the course. The team stayed the course. Of course, over a long period of time, lots of things can change, which is why we keep time limited or fixed here.

R = 0 to 100%: 0 means the team has nothing (no tools, no time, no skills, no equipment, no training, etc.). 100% means the teams has access to all necessary tools to get the job done most efficiently. They are NOT starved for anything. The team has done their homework, has appropriate equipment, skills, etc. as needed and is correctly prepared for a development cycle.

A = 0 to 100%: 0 means the team and other stakeholders just don't care about being accountable or that no measurements are taking place. Remember that measurement is an actual service that you provide as a leader. 100% means the team holds itself accountable, and they know the stakeholders will as well, because there are clear, ideally agreed-upon, measures in place.

P = 0 to 100%: 0 means the team is easily distracting itself by working on interesting side or pet projects, or stakeholders are coming in every hour and asking the team for something. Distractions pour in from a fire hose. 100% means the team stands up for itself. It is willing and knows how to say, "no" to distractions. It means everyone (team and stakeholders) are focused on delivering the goals set forth for the development period, and no one is distracting them.

r = 0 to 100%: 0 means the team doesn't respect itself at all and is willing to let stakeholders run roughshod all over them. It means teammates will openly complain about other teammates in the hallway or over their cubicle walls, regardless if everyone hears them. It also means stakeholders could care less about the team, not only in a development period, but as people who deserve common respect and the ability to do meaningful work. 100% means there are no internal politics or disrespect among members in the team. It means the organization is not tumultuous with political distractions.

You can roughly figure out the number to plug into the equation by taking the number of people who are affected and divide that by the total number of people on the team. For example, if you have a 10 person team and one person is always getting pulled into side projects you can estimate protection as 9/10 or 90%. You may be tempted to dig deeper and bring in the percent of time this person is distracted, but don't do so. The formula should be used as a high-level guide for the conversation, not as a mind-numbing exercise in math.

Let's see some examples to exercise the model.

Example 1: Extreme Lows

```
C = 0%D*(0%R+0%A+0%M+0%P+0%r)/5
= 0% Commitment.
```

This says, the project is nothing more than a twinkle in someone's eye. It's just an idea. There are no resources (money, time, people, or equipment) dedicated to it, no direction, no accountability, no rewards, and no protection. Therefore no one has committed anything.

Example 2: Extreme Highs

```
C                                         =
100%D*(100%R+100%A+100%M+100%P+100%r)/5
= 100% Commitment.
```

This says, we are living in an entirely ideal world, where all things that feed into commitment are perfect, and therefore the team can commit 100% too. Is it possible? I've never seen it.

Example 3: A Challenged Team

```
C = 50%D*(100%R+50%A+50%M+50%P+60%r)/5
= 31% Commitment.
```

D = 50%	This says the project has some direction that significantly changed halfway through the development period, or that the design documentation is "half-baked" at best, causing lots of confusion and rework.
R = 100%	The project has all the resources it needs
A = 50%	The team half-heartedly hold themselves accountable to deliver on the goal by the end of the period. No one is measuring anything in earnest.
M = 50%	Personal motivations are partially aligned with what is being asked. The people are half-in, half-out. No one is proactively encouraging them to forge ahead.
P = 50%	The team is only partially protected from

	outside requests. Some of the team is doing "nice-guy tasks" or "hallway asks" from other stakeholders.
r = 60%	Respect is low. People are bickering at each other, or politics are going on behind closed doors. No on may be saying thank you in a genuine way.
C = 31%	We can interpret this in a few ways:

1. The chances are about 31% (or 1 in 3) the team will deliver everything they said they would.
2. Only 3 out of 10 people on your team are fully committed.
3. All the people on your team are fed up and don't care what happens by the end of the development period. They have a "yeah, whatever" attitude and may actually slip the deadline altogether.

However, you choose to describe the results, you should notice how powerful the multiplier effect on commitment is that comes from inconsistent or unclear direction. When several of the inputs are half-hearted, commitment plummets towards zero.

Example 4: Realistic Success

```
C = 100%D*(100%R+90%A+90%M+90%P+100%r)/5
  = 94% Commitment.
```

D = 100%	This says the project has crystal clear direction that won't change over the commitment period.
R = 100%	The project has all the resources it needs
A = 90%	Most of the team holds itself accountable. Someone is providing the service of measuring progress, giving the team clarity on how they are doing.
M = 90%	Personal motivations are mostly aligned with what is being asked, and the team is regularly encouraged to stay on task.
P = 90%	The team is mostly protected from outside requests.
r = 100%	Respect is high. There is no conflict between peers and no politics going on behind the scenes.
C = 94%	Chances are the project will land with about 94% of the committed work done. Said another way, the project has 15 out of 16 chances everything will get done by the end of the development period.

In this scenario, depending on how strongly the team feels about staying on track, some teammates may do a little more work than usual to land everything, which essentially means they are making up the lost time caused by distractions and unforeseen problems. That's fine, and this commitment level may come from a high level of respect for other persons on the team, personal motivations to succeed, integrity, etc...

Example 5: Uncontrollable Variables

Here's a real-world situation faced by a mobile development team with a very successful, several years old mobile game that is based on a licensed property.

They're quite good at execution. According to their leadership, they've never missed a deadline. They rarely have overtime, except in the case where their licensor delivered approvals late in the cycle. One of their producers put it well when he said, "[That licensor] is a variable out of our control." He described how complicated the licensor's world was and said they simply had to put the game team's needs lower than other priorities.

In terms of the formula, this means there is no way to 100% protect the team from tardy input or late requests to tweak the direction.

The leadership and team made peace with this challenging situation by working the best way they knew how to accommodate this perpetually late and unpredictable resource on their team. It wasn't perfect, and it did damage the team's ability to commit.

The team grew quiet in its opinions about what to do, and the team's sense of ownership dropped. They still delivered a high-quality game, because they figured out how to work around the issue. They knew every once in a while, they would work a late evening or weekend to catch up with changes, if the licensor came back very late with change requests.

Here's what the formula looked like:

```
C = 95%D*(100%R+100%A+75%M+50%P+100%r)/5

  = 81% Commitment.
```

D = 95%	Overall, the team had a mostly consistent direction, but the licensor would occasionally provide tardy feedback that changed the direction.
R = 100%	The project had all the resources it needed.
A = 90%	The team held itself accountable for producing a quality game.
M = 75%	Personal motivations were mostly aligned with the goal, but the team's challenges represented a constant, low-level drain on morale.
P = 50%	The team could not be completely protected from late input from the licensor, which was a chronic issue.
r = 100%	Respect was high. They had been working together for several years, had mutual respect, and had gotten into a non-stressful development relationship with each other.
C = 81%	The team did the best they could in the situation they found themselves in. They will never be able to deliver perfectly every time, but they consistently come close and roll with the punches well enough to execute.

The constant uncontrollable partner drained the morale of the team, but they still delivered. They still committed. The changing direction from this licensor was infrequent enough not to destroy the team's overall ability to move ahead. It just put a constant, low level drain on their morale over time. Leadership also explained what was going on to the team, and in doing so, helped the team to better handle the frustrations and stress that came from such an arrangement. Not a perfect situation, but not bad either.

Using the Formula

Of course, you can explain the egg and stool metaphor to your team and the product owners, VPs, and CEOs interacting with your team. However, the DRAMPr formula gives you a shorthand to quickly communicate just how much of an impact their actions have on the team.

For example, say you have someone who is constantly coming to your team asking for side-projects or favors. Here's how you can use the formula to quickly get your point across. Take them a whiteboard, write down the formula, explain the P variable, and show him or her how a low level of protection is damaging the team's ability to commit.

You'll write it like this:
```
C = D(R+A+M+P+r)/5
C = 100%D*(100%R+100%A+100%M+10%P+100%r)/5
C = 82% Commitment.
```

You can say it like this: "We've been working on a methodical approach to get the team's maximum commitment during this period. We want to be at 100%. Unfortunately, by frequently asking for changes during this period, you are damaging the team's ability to deliver on their commitments. We may only get 82% of the features we're trying to ship this quarter. Plus, the team will eventually stop committing altogether; that's really scary for us. Can you do your part to help us protect them by not placing outside asks on them? That will really help us keep the team committed to delivering the product as quickly as possible. Let's take the new idea you have and put it in their future work for next time."

Shared Staff

Coming together is a beginning. Keeping together is progress. Working together is success. – Henry Ford

Often, software companies will make two or three products or have a set of central teams. At various points in their development cycles, companies will share employees between two or more teams. Cultural differences can grow between central teams and ones that directly deliver a product to market or deliver a service contract to a customer. There are also challenges in sharing staff among multiple teams. This chapter is designed to help you to manage staff among multiple teams and to ensure they are able to commit to those teams.

First, a central team is usually a group of staff that work on shared technologies many groups within the company use. The shared technologies may be products that have been grown over time by the company, such as a UI technology stack, telemetry tools, or runtime renderers such as those in games or 3D training tools database tools. Those tools are created in-house to save time. They eventually have enough momentum to need their own staff to maintain and grow the tools, so the company can maintain a competitive advantage in getting to market more quickly or more efficiently.

Sometimes those internal tools are also seen as something that can be productized and sold externally. This is very common, and I just tend to call it a "consult to product" business model. Turning an internal toolset into a market-facing product helps to smooth out the revenue ups and down of a services company by generating licensed sales or monthly revenues if you have a Software as a Service (SaaS) model. So, that's how central teams and product teams can evolve from services companies.

What naturally happens is that the central teams, especially the ones that are not directly shipping product to customers or performing services to customers, end up having a different culture than the ones that are "on the front lines." The central teams often have a more even work/life balance, making them a bit envied by the services teams who often are grinding to hit an approaching deadline.

The central teams can control their backlogs of work, get a very stable series of sprints, and can work much more closely to the idealized agile model the world of Scrum development has come to know and love. Those developing products against a major market deadline or a major customer deadline on a fixed price contract often don't have that luxury.

Those shipping products are under market pressure to deliver "back of the box" features at acceptable value. If they fail, they risk getting bad reviews and taking on brand damage. Those delivering consulting services under a contract are under pressure to deliver several more features that have crept in over time or that grew in scope due to a lack of understanding in the early days of the project. Either way, they rarely get full control over their backlogs and smoothly running sprints. As deadlines approach, things get worse, and hours go up.

If the central team is simply delivering internal tools, they are seen as a cost center. They don't directly make the company money; they simply save it. That means their salaries are being paid by those delivering products to market or those working on contracts. Similarly, a product team formed in the early or pre-revenue days of the product is also a cost center. Their product is not yet profitable, so they are costing the company more money than they are making. That is considered an investment by the company.

Challenge #1: Morale During Relocation

In tough periods where a services team or a product is significantly behind schedule, managers will raise their hand and ask for central team members. The idea is the business needs to sacrifice a little long-term gain for the short-term crisis. This makes sense for the business, as after all, you must serve your customers in order to stay in business long enough to deliver the next features in those central tools or products.

The challenge on a personal level is introduced when the central team members on those teams get pulled onto the "front line" teams. Many individual employees don't understand how the business works. They assume money is coming in from somewhere and never really understand that sales of software or services directly lead to their salaries. So, if you are managing a business or a central team with a wall of natural protection around it for most of the year, and you then tell someone they are being pulled (even temporarily) onto a front-line team, you may have a challenge keeping their morale high. They may feel mistreated and see being pulled onto a front-line team as a regression in their careers. They may fear not being put back on their central team. They may fear the long hours on the front-line teams. They may have other fears, such as losing their skillsets, based on whether the front-line teams use more tools instead of coding. On some level, they may simply feel that this reallocation of their time is unfair.

So, how do you handle keeping those members motivated during the shared staffing situation? And how do you ensure they can commit to the front-line team?

If you face morale drop, have a one on one meeting with each employee. Discuss how money flows through the business and explain by being on a central team (or on a product team that has yet to be significantly profitable) they are costing the company money. Confirm with them that you would also prefer to take the long view and have them stay on the central team, which will inevitably solve problems across the company and for many teams instead of just one team. Then explain to them the profits from the front-line team pays their salary. Explain in order for the business to stay alive long enough to get those new central team features into reality, the company first needs to pay all its bills, including their salary. Explain you understand the situation is not ideal, but joining the front-line team is absolutely critical to the ongoing success of the company, and that once they get over the milestone or delivery that has caused the need for shared-staffing, the employee and organization will be able to return to normal. They'll pick right back up making central tools or product features.

Challenge #2: Incomplete Visibility

When an employee is shared across two programs, it is harder to see that they are fully booked on both programs, since you can't see everything they are doing. How do you keep them from blowing a commitment on your team, because their other team hit a snag and needed more time?

When you don't have visibility over 100% of the staff member's schedule, just plan to have a regular talk with them and their other leader. Agree on the number of hours you have from that staff member on your team. Be vigilant about getting accurate estimates from him or her before work commitments are made for the next time period (two to four weeks in Scrum), and actively hold them accountable in meetings in front of the team and privately, when needed, if they start to slip their deadlines.

Be honest and professional, that you expect them to deliver on their commitments, since you have worked so hard to facilitate those commitments. If they keep missing the delivery of their commitments to you, book a meeting with them, their career manager, and perhaps other leaders as needed, and politely ask for help. Often times, when programs are sharing staff, communications are poor between programs, and neither of its leaders really know what to expect. A quick meeting here and there can clear things up both for you, and most importantly, for the employee.

Challenge #3: Balancing Customer Support Needs

Protecting the team from the randomization that comes from supporting customers is another challenge of software development with a product team. Whether the product team is a central team supporting service teams in a large company or it is a customer-facing product team supporting customers out in the field, it can be challenging to keep commitments when customers have a spike in support needs. To handle this, you can allocate a lower percentage of the staff's time, such as 50% to the product development effort each sprint or each release period and 50% to covering support. You'll be able to cover spikes in support when needed, and you'll be able to get "bonus features" done when support is low. This may seem trivial, but it goes a long way to keeping a better morale by regularly serving up wins instead of losses.

As a Leader Training Your Culture

You are your greatest asset. Put your time, effort and money into training, grooming, and encouraging your greatest asset.
-Tom Hopkins

As a leader transforming your culture, you must instill the concepts into all of your organization for it to work. Here are tips you can follow to ensure your culture understands, embraces, and carries on this healthy paradigm even when you are not there and, hopefully, even after you leave.

1. Make commitment a core value in your company. Although C-level leaders or founders enjoy the privilege of writing the values of an entire organization, you can still ensure *your* team understands commitment is a critical concept.

2. Follow this method yourself. Be the champion in the company. Mention the key concepts from time to time, so people are reminded you are serious about keeping a healthy culture that they can trust and depend on.

3. Seek feedback. Every now and again bring it up in a presentation as a simple health assessment. Ask the team to perform health surveys to check on whether all legs of the stool, the seat, fortifiers, and the clear coat are working. Ensure you know what the team feels by using this simple metaphor to help them articulate their feedback. As an example, say, "Are any of the legs on our stool short lately? If

so, why?" You can accomplish this with a simple (and usually free) survey tool, like Survey Monkey.

4. Build support among your leadership. Set expectations you are very interested in improving the health of the team (as it directly affects the bottom line). Ask them to understand the concepts, discuss them with you, and gather feedback using them.

5. If you truly intend to change your team culture or your entire company culture, you must think in terms of mentorship or apprenticeship. You must weave in bits of this process and this mindset into your culture in various areas to ensure it sinks in and changes all of the organization. You cannot do it alone. The fastest way to ensure your culture changes is to give your teams the tools they need to push these concepts into the rest of the organization.

6. Train new hires on the concept. As a part of their ramp-up, incorporate this book (or something like it) as part of their training. A new hire second-guesses their decision to join an organization the most during their first month. They are watching to see if they are a good fit, if the company is a good fit, and whether their manager is engaged with their well-being in mind. The concepts in this book will put their minds at ease.

7. Listen for misinterpretations and fix them in one-on-one conversations. It is easy for many management paradigms to

be misinterpreted or partially implemented. Although this egg and stool concept is rather simple, it is still at risk of these pitfalls.

8. Create a policy that supports this cultural health awareness as a requirement. For example, in annual reviews, have employees document one action they took in the past year to strengthen one of the legs (or the seat, if they are a leader). When the metaphor is used right in annual reviews, it will be a clear indicator of how seriously you regard cultural health on the team. By holding the employees responsible for supporting and contributing to that culture, you are empowering your organization to live and breathe good cultural practices.

9. Celebrate when the team demonstrates it is getting healthier. Have a party when your team health surveys come back showing success. Visualize the metaphor for them.

10. When the culture is hurting and not meeting the goals of the metaphor, ask the team to develop a plan to solve the problem. People will surprise you with solutions when they know you care, and they know they have a say in how to achieve a goal.

Stacking and Managing Individuals

"If I have seen further, it is by standing on the shoulders of giants." – Sir Isaac Newton

Organizations are built of teams. Teams are built of individuals. Ultimately the health of the organization depends on the health of the teams.

For example, imagine each member of your team has a stool that represents their commitment to the team. Now, imagine stacking those stools to form a pyramid. If everyone's stool is strong and sturdy, the pyramid will be sturdy too. If there are stools that are weak or missing legs, the pyramid is weakened. With too many weak stools, no matter how much time you put into your overall culture, the pyramid will fall. i.e. The corporation will suffer.

This approach to the metaphor reminds managers that attending to the individual needs of their teammates is required in order to build a stronger team. It may seem obvious, but like so many topics covered in this book, and like so many things a manager knows he or she should do, this one often gets left at a lower priority than other items on a leader's to do list. It is often overlooked until there is a problem. It is often even neglected or completely misunderstood by managers who are either undertrained, inappropriately promoted, or poorly matched with their teammates (in the case of multi-disciplinary teams).

If you are a manager, look at your relationship with every teammate you manage from the commitment lens. This will ensure you are building trust with that person on a regular basis. Do they understand the direction of their career and where the team is headed? Do they have the correct resources for their role? Are they protected from confusion and held accountable against their commitments? And most importantly, do you have mutual respect for each other? If you are managing someone who you don't respect or who doesn't respect you, that's a sure-fire path to them leaving.

Most of this comes down to both of you consciously seeking ways to bond with each other. For managers, your regular one-on-ones are your opportunity to dig deeper and verify you are meeting your teammates' needs on all aspects. If you are ever tempted to start out a one-on-one by saying, "What do you want to discuss, this is *your* time?" to your teammate, hold that thought. That puts them on the defensive, makes them feel responsible, and can quickly lead to a failed opportunity.

If you are dreading the one-on-ones, you haven't done a good job of preparation, or as often is the case, the teammate isn't holding up their end of the bargain. Obviously once you have worked with someone for a long time, it becomes less about getting access to the shallow info and more about day-to-day bonding. There will also be times when you have spoken so much that you don't need a sync-up. There is nothing wrong with canceling one every now and again. But you can sense when you are canceling them more to avoid meeting with the person than just because you are already caught up. That's a great indicator you need to work on building their stool with them. In this case, map out their stool, look for weaknesses and opportunities to fortify. Ask them to do the same thing independently. Compare notes. This will make your syncs more meaningful and will freshen the relationship when needed.

If you are an individual, recognize you are responsible for your own stool. Recognize your manager is there to help you and that by actively working to engage him or her, you are building the bonds necessary for your own success. However, your manager is not in control of your destiny. You are. Don't be a leaf on the wind, thinking your manager and company will take care of you. You must actively participate.

I am a huge fan of framing my teammate's reference for their position on a team in terms of their personal brands. Along the lines of the "company of one" concept, I set their expectations on how their actions, attitudes, work performance, etc. contribute to their personal brands in their company or team. I often share with them insights they can't see themselves, as people aren't always forthright with how they view you. But as a manager, I have access to "the grapevine" and subjective feedback from their peers and other managers. I explain how they can manage their personal brands, change them for the better, and use those insights to guide their careers within the organization.

Recognize you have an opportunity to leverage your manager's access to information you can't get on your own. If you are serious about owning your own career, build a rapport with your manager, as awkward as it may feel at times, so you can get the help and insights you need when you need them. Use the egg & stool metaphor to ask for their guidance, and to hold your managers accountable for guiding you. That doesn't mean you need to be rude. That's the worst way to build a trusting relationship. Be honest and humble.

Here's an example. "You know, I was thinking more on this whole egg & stool metaphor for building a good culture and ensuring I have a great home here at Company X. I'm worried though, I'm getting a bit scattered by the different requests coming in. I really want to help execute on the team's plan, but I don't feel as efficient with those other tasks, such as, (name the ones that aren't working for you). Is it possible somehow for you and me to prioritize those against the main plan, and perhaps shelve the ones distracting me? I'd love to get back to 100% efficiency as soon as possible."

The above simply follows a basic "I statements" formula often discussed in relationship and communications books, that goes like this: "When you do X, it makes me feel Y, I would like to Z." It applies the "I statement" formula to a scenario where your manager may not be protecting you. What's worse, they may be the one randomizing you, and they don't even realize it.

The stronger your manager-to-teammate relationship is, the more you will trust each other. The more teammates trust their managers, and each other, the stronger the team will be. The stronger the teams, the stronger the company. The more people will lean on each other, have respect for each other, and execute well with each other. The pyramid of stools will be stronger for it.

Wear and Tear

"I like fixing things," he said as he worked. "The world is always breaking, here and there, this way and that. Fix a bit of it, and I feel like I'm helping." – Bruce Coville

Stools get old and fall into disrepair. So, can a culture. How do you handle *keeping* your stool strong and trustable?

When it comes to company culture, we must remember organizations are living entities. They're always changing, either moving ahead or backwards, and most certainly seeing an influx of new faces and then an outflux of old faces. People may want to do something different after a while and leave. Some people get set in their ways. Some people get frustrated. Some people get bored. But no matter what the reason, the face of the organization changes regularly.

Despite even your best efforts at creating a great culture, people will move on. Those who stay can become complacent. You can be complacent, if you are not careful. Complacency will most assuredly work against the health of the organizational culture. People naturally fall into bad habits. They may stop communicating as well as they used to, or they forget some of the things you taught them. They may forget the value of self-coordination. They may slip in a few side-projects here or there and eventually erode the concept of protection. Each one of the legs in your stool can get old and worn out.

What happens when people become more senior? Do they feel like they should no longer be held accountable? Are new junior members join too intimidated to hold senior people accountable? If you leave and another leader comes in, will your culture withstand that transition?

The answer to whether your culture is strong enough for the next leader to keep it going depends on how well you have maintained your stool over the years and how well you have ensured the culture you are building is also built by the team. Cultural changes only happen when the team buys in.

Even bad cultural changes are the result of the team buying into them. When a team slowly slides into a worn and torn culture, they are unconsciously buying into it. Most of them would deny it, if you asked them whether they supported a culture getting less committed week by week. People inherently want to do the right thing, and they try to. However, when times get tough, such as when leadership is making mistakes, poor economics occur, or the team has poor resources, people justify their behaviors and blame external causes. Sometimes the external causes really *are* to blame. If someone is not constantly polishing the stool, adding a little glue here to repair it, sanding it down, and adding new stain or new paint, the stool will get old. It will get rickety. It will eventually break.

Cultures are not easy to build, and they are hard to maintain. When market pressures force people to make tough decisions, they often sacrifice cultural boundaries in order to deliver product to market. They make a short-term sacrifice for a short-term gain, which eventually leads to a long-term degradation of their values.

Creating a plan to start improving your culture for the better is not a "one and done" scenario. You may have some significant changes to make in the beginning. You may have some significant selling to do to encourage your team to buy in to what you are trying to accomplish. Not everyone will understand. Not everyone will care. It will be your job to help sell your ideas into the organization in a way that makes the individuals care. Once you have done this, and you see the improvements happening in the organization, you cannot stop there. You must continue to build in processes around the major legs of your stool and the fortifiers you care about, so that the culture extends past your tenure at the organization.

Often, mission statements and value statements are used as mechanisms by founders or C level management of organizations to help set the culture of their companies. Mission statements and value statements are one way to simplify cultural encouragement to your organization across multiple locations and multiple societal cultures. But what I'm describing is more about staying involved with the maintenance of your culture than simply stating it.

This is particularly true when everyone is running out of time, there are pressures to get your product to market, you are running low on money etc. When those large distractions come in, it is fine to focus your attention on them. But remind yourself to come back. Remind yourself that maintaining the stool is critical to the long-term success of your organization. It is critical to your culture to keep people feeling healthy and feeling connected. It is critical to their trusting your organization for the long term.

If you start with people first, you will build a culture that lasts as long as possible. If you're constantly watching the major legs of the stool in your organization, you'll be able to tell if one is starting to get weak and needs strengthening. If you are watching the direction, you can tell if that seat is twisting too much or tilting too much, resulting in a sloppy direction for your team to follow. All of these things come together under your leadership to ensure your team stays healthy and unified.

Don't forget to get out your stool, get out the glue, get out the sanding paper, and stain or paint, and level every few months to see how that stool is doing. Watch your culture. To bring the metaphor to reality a moment, if you ship an annual product, or on some other recurring cycle, build in training days, and cultural reassessment days at the end of each launch period. Don't let the need to "get ahead" on the next release stop your team from taking a moment to fix their faux pas. To clean up the mess. To do a postmortem. To recommit. If they regularly recommit to the values, you will maintain a healthy culture.

Change is OK

A favorite mentor of mine used to tell me about his grandfather's axe. He would say, "This is my grandfather's axe. I've changed the handle and I've changed the blade, but it is still my grandfather's axe."

My takeaway from his metaphor was that no matter how you might change the components of an overall system, it is still your system. That is true for your culture as well. Times do change, and companies must change too.

For example, industrial age companies used pension plans to entice employees to stay (potentially for the entirety of their careers). Then in the 70's, companies recognized what a terrible idea this was. They could not sustain the older population for decades after those people retired. So, companies switched to the 401K common in corporate retirement plans today.

That is an example of a large-scale fortifier that changed. As times changed, and people recognized they could no longer trust companies that said they could deliver on pension commitments, companies changed to 401Ks. Even though they had to change, companies still kept their culture of taking care of their employees intact[1].

You can do the same thing. Know when to change your stool's struts. The legs and the seat must stay intact, but your fortifiers can change as you see fit over time to meet the changing needs of the people on your team and the world within which you operate.

---

[1] Check out Robert Kiyosaki's book, *Cash Flow Quadrant,* to learn more about this transition.

When People Put Their Feet Down

Say something, I'm giving up on you.
- Ian Axel and Chad King

In 1991, John Meyer and Natalie Allen published their Three Component Model of Commitment in the "Human Resource Management Review". This model discussed the three types of commitment that will drive someone to stay with your organization. They are affection for your company, fear of loss, and a sense of obligation. Affection describes how loyal and attached they are to your organization. Fear of loss, as it implies, describes what they will perceive losing should they leave your company, such as title, a level of pay, etc. Sense of obligation describes how strongly their personal code of honor pushes them to stay with you, because "it's the right thing to do."

Remembering the extension of the metaphor in the chapter called "Fortifiers", we discussed that people can raise their feet and more fully commit to your stool (stay at your company). The opposite can occur too, and sometimes you can see it coming.

When people put their feet down off of your stool, you can tell in body language, affect, and demeanor, that something is changing. When people completely get off the stool, which means they are leaving the company, the reasons they left are usually obvious looking back.

If you are a manager, and you are concerned someone may be putting their feet down, then you can do a better job with their stool.

Refer to the section on stacking. People's body language, and frankly sometimes just what they say, if things have gotten bad enough, are indicators they are thinking of leaving, or at least that they just don't trust you.

If you are an individual, and you are unhappy with your situation at work, do some self-exploration to find out why. Read the stacking section in this book. Before you choose to leave, see if you can repair the situation with your manager - that is if you care enough about the job. If that doesn't work, see if there is another manager you can ask for help. Perhaps with a little collaboration to explore and fix problems, you can turn a frustrating situation into a positive one.

I'd like to also offer a bit of related advice to those of you who are young in your careers or just starting them. If at all possible, ask to meet your future managers during job interviews. Be polite but persistent. Your manager will have the largest effect on your time with that organization, so you'll do yourself and the company a large favor in checking compatibility with that person before joining the team. When you do meet them, ask what they like to see from their employees and how they like to manage. Ask if there is anything they really don't like and whether they know of any mentoring for you that happens while you are there. You can gather a sense of how it would be to work with them.

Recall that the egg and stool are a metaphor to help you build commitment. The Meyer and Allen model is a way of understanding what affects your teammates' decisions to stay or leave. Use the stool to proactively build affection commitment to keep your team around for the long term and for the right reasons.

A Call to Action

Vision without action is merely a dream. Action without vision just passes the time. Vision with action can change the world.
  -Joel A. Barker

You read this book because you are looking for something. If you are looking for a solution to a cultural problem that feels like a lack of commitment, I hope you've found an answer you can identify with. If you are simply trying to further your understanding of how to get commitment from your teammates, I hope you've found some tools you are comfortable using.

Now it is time for you to act. Your team, your organization, and your company will thank you for it. They may not outright shake your hand and pat you on the back, but they *will* improve productivity, be healthier and happier, view the company or team in a better light, and ...*stay*.

They will have a reason to stay, even when times get hard for the company. If you do nothing else, write these tenants in a letter to your team, use the survey in the Tools at the end of this book, and get the conversation going. You can even make a Commitment Contract with yourself to make this happen. The Commitment Contract and other tools to help you are also located in the Tools section at the end of this book.

In "The E Myth", a book on entrepreneurship, Michael Gerber teaches that you should envision how your final company operates and how it impacts your life, and then use every day to drive your company in that direction. I agree. Anything left to chance alone has a great chance of failing. Envision and build your culture against a plan, so it has a real chance of success.

Help your team to help themselves, and it will grow from there. Build commitment one leg at a time and make a difference.

Tools

What follows is a set of tactical tools you can use to drive a commitment culture in your organization. They consist of:

- Templates to drive commitment
- Surveys to gauge commitment
- A contract to proactively discuss the pieces of commitment with your team

A Value Template

It's the job of any business owner to be clear about the company's nonnegotiable core values. They're the riverbanks that help guide us as we refine and improve on performance and excellence. A lack of riverbanks creates estuaries and cloudy waters that are confusing to navigate. I want a crystal-clear, swiftly flowing stream. - Danny Meyer

To help you lead your company with a culture of commitment, I have written the commitment value template below and some instructions on how you can revisit it regularly with employees to sew those seeds of commitment. Copy and paste this directly into your values.

Value: Commitment. At (Your Company), we value leaders and teammates who stay committed. We give our people the appropriate resources, protection, direction, and respect to reach our goals. We strive to align their motivations with ours while holding them accountable with measurement to deliver great work. The result is that we achieve a high level of excellence for our organization which makes us stronger in any market we approach.

Here's a template that you can use for every annual review. Have the employee fill out this statement:

In order to hold up the Commitment value, I have done the following thing(s): *(Each employee fills this in. Please choose one or more below.) Describe how you…*

- provided or asked for appropriate resources, protection, or direction.
- gained respect from, or grew respect for, a colleague.
- explored my own personal motivations to see how they align with what the business is asking of me.
- held someone accountable or held myself accountable when needed.
- showed commitment to my company
- showed commitment to my team

Building this into one of your key values ensures your organization is building trust from the ground up. Building it into the annual reviews ensures people are keeping this value template in mind driving their weekly work, where it means the most.

This format works for individual contributors and for managers. Just tailor as needed. Note people can also set personal growth goals. If as a manager you notice a teammate is failing to show respect to others or is clearly not performing well at self-protection, ask them to set that as one of the annual review goals. As an individual, you can offer this as a personal goal to your manager and ask for their support.

Surveys

Below is a sample survey that you can share with your team to get a sense of how much they trust your organization. This can be a first step, or "litmus test" to see how far away you are from the high-quality standards of a commitment culture. An updated version of this quiz is available at MasteringCommitment.com. You are also welcome to add it to your own survey via free survey tools like Survey Monkey.

On a scale of 1 to 5, where 1 is strongly disagree, 2 is disagree, 3 is neither agree nor disagree, 4 is agree and 5 is strongly agree, please choose which level correctly matches your level of agreement with each sentence below:

Core Tenants of Commitment:

Direction:
I believe my team knows exactly what we are supposed to do at any given time.
I believe my team knows exactly where we are headed over the next year.
I know exactly what is expected of me in order to do the best job I can do.
My leaders give very consistent direction, without significant change.

Resources:

I have everything that I need to do my job most effectively.

My team has everything that it needs to do its job most effectively.

When our team needs something, our leadership quickly gets us what we need in order to do our job effectively.

Accountability:

My leadership fully expects me to deliver on all of my commitments at the end of our development period.

We track clear metrics on our program, so we know how well we are doing.

At any point, my leader and I know exactly how close I have gotten to achieving my goals for the period.

Our team regularly delivers on all of our commitments at the end of our development period.

I am generally able to deliver on all of my estimated work by the end of a development period.

Motivation:

My financial needs are being met here.

My career needs are being met here.

I feel a high level of autonomy in my work.

I am not micromanaged.

I am learning about or mastering something of value.

while working on this effort.

I have a sense of purpose here.

Protection:

In any given development cycle, our team is able to stay focused on our commitments and avoid any distractions from the outside.

In any given development cycle, I am an able to stay focused, and I don't get distracted working on things outside of my commitments.

In any given development cycle, no one comes up to me and asks for favors or tasks outside the ones I have already committed to.

Respect:

I respect my boss.

My boss respects me.

I respect all of my teammates.

All of my teammates respect me.

My company respects my role in this organization.

Fortifiers:

Communications:

We use email very effectively to get our jobs done.

We use meetings very effectively to get our jobs done.

We use documentation very effectively to get our jobs done.

We use our project management tools very effectively to get our jobs done.

Training:

My on-the-job training has been very effective in preparing me to do a better job.

Our team wide training has been very effective in helping us to do a better job.

My company or team clearly invests in regular training so that we can do a better job.

Ramp-up:

Our ramp-up documentation and process need no improvement.

Our ramp-up and documentation process affectively get our new hires integrated into our team as quickly as possible.

Our leadership makes it clear that they value a good community-driven ramp up process for new hires.

Team Building:

Our team building exercises occur regularly.

Our team building exercises are effective at helping me to get to know my teammates.

Our team building exercises are effective at helping me to get to know my leadership.

I feel like a critical part of my team.

You can also add other fortifiers to your survey listings.

Results:

Overall Trust:

I trust my leadership to care about me and my personal needs.

I trust my leadership to care about my career moving forward.

I trust my leadership to care about my personal growth.

I trust that my teammates are doing the best job they can.

I trust my organization will look out for me when times get hard.

Turnover:

I do not plan to leave this organization anytime soon.

Should I decide to leave this organization, I will first talk with my leaders to share why I want to leave and give them an opportunity to help me resolve my concerns and stay.

I have no reason that would make me want to leave this organization.

I have no reason that would make me want to stay.

I like my company.

I like my boss.

Commitment:

I have everything I need to fully commit to delivering my work on time.

I am ready to work more hours here and there to ensure I meet my commitments.

I often do work more hours than expected to ensure I meet my commitments.

This organization gives me no compelling reasons to work more than a normal work week.

I like my:

- company more than my team.
- team more than my company.
- company and team the same.

The Commitment Contract

When I write a goal down - and I truly write them down - it becomes a part of me. That's a contract that I sign with myself to say, 'I don't care what happens - I'm going to stay on this path. I'm going to try and see this through; I'm going to give it my best shot, my best effort. - Gail Devers

I personally prefer books that give me very tactical solutions after explaining the academic reasoning or strategy behind their books. In the spirit of this, I am giving you another tool besides the survey. The survey is intended to gauge commitment, so you can find problems and fix them. This tool, the Commitment Contract, is intended to help you facilitate a conversation with those people from whom you are trying to get commitment. It also ensures you remember to deliver on your parts of the commitment too.

This contract captures all the pieces in the metaphor in one place. It is a simple fill-in-the blank you can photocopy from the book any time you are trying to gain genuine commitment. I confess I use this with myself, when I am trying to hold myself accountable for doing personal things like improve some behavior of mine that I don't like as a leader, a parent, a spouse, etc. We are all imperfect, and we can all improve. Writing things down helps to make commitments crystal clear.

I encourage you to try it a few times. Copy it, fill it out, and put it on your wall, where you can see it daily. I even like to keep a tally on the back of the sheet for how many times I have been successful or failed to keep my personal commitments with it, as a reminder that I am still committed to the goal. With your team, print it out for each of them. Recall that although we work as a team, commitment is a personal thing. Management Psychologist, William Horst told me of research that says when people verbally commit to something, they are significantly more likely to follow through. I also know that entrepreneurs are able to secure confidence from investors when they produce letters of intent or actual contracts. I believe that by writing things down, seeking clarity on assumptions, we facilitate the things necessary to drive true commitment. You can download a copy at chrisharden.com/masteringcommitment/supplements.

Print it. Try it. Practice it.

Commitment Contract

I commit to:
_____
_____
_____
(Goal/Direction)

until or by _____
(Date)

if I am able to receive or find the following items from _____
_____ that are required to support my commitment:

1. Consistent, Clear Direction (what is stated above does not change)

2. Resources:
_____
_____

    Protections:
_____
_____

3. Motivations:
_____
_____

4. Respect and support.

5. And that you will help me stay accountable with these measurements:
_____
_____

If during this time, direction changes so much that I feel less committed, we'll review and may update or cancel this contract.

　　Signed: _____

　　Dated: _____

(© 2019 Chris Harden, from "Mastering Commitment")

A Request

If you found value in this book, please leave a review on Amazon. This will help other customers evaluate the potential of this book for themselves and encourage Amazon to show it to like-minded readers.

Dedication

To Laurie, Asher, and Finley, you are my inspiration for everything. To you, I commit to be the best father and husband I can be.

- Chris

Special Thanks

Steven Yee
David Ewing
Meir Wasserman
Jeremy Scheinberg
Eric Chrisman
Dani Alcorn
Bill Horst

www.ingramcontent.com/pod-product-compliance
Lightning Source LLC
Chambersburg PA
CBHW060839220526
45466CB00003B/1167